BEING BINKY

BEING BINKY

Binky Felstead

**SIMON &
SCHUSTER**

London · New York · Sydney · Toronto · New Delhi

A CBS COMPANY

To my late grandmother, Ba Ba, who was
the quirkiest, most amazing and loving granny
anyone could ever wish for

First published in Great Britain by Simon & Schuster UK Ltd, 2014
This paperback edition published by Simon & Schuster UK Ltd, 2015
A CBS COMPANY

3 5 7 9 10 8 6 4

Simon & Schuster UK Ltd
1st Floor
222 Gray's Inn Road
London WC1X 8HB

www.simonandschuster.co.uk

Simon & Schuster Australia, Sydney
Simon & Schuster India, New Delhi

A CIP catalogue record for this book
is available from the British Library

ISBN: 978-1-47113-458-6
ebook ISBN: 978-1-47113-459-3

Typeset in the UK by M Rules
Printed and bound by CPI Group (UK) Ltd, Croydon, CR0 4YY

CONTENTS

PROLOGUE

The winter sun was streaming through the window of Ollie Locke's beaten-up Ford as we sped along the Thames Embankment. It was late 2010 and we were heading back to our flats in Fulham. We were about to star in a new reality show about people who lived in Chelsea, and we were slightly giggly and hysterical at the thought that we were actually going to be on TV.

'Can you imagine someone asking us for our pictures?' I pondered. The idea seemed completely ridiculous.

'What about fans hanging outside our houses hoping to meet us or ask for our autograph? Can you actually imagine that?' someone else chipped in. Cheska Hull and I, who were flatmates at the time, were squashed in the back of the car, while our friend Ollie was driving and his flatmate, Alex Brocket, was next to him in the front.

'Darling, it's going be fabulous,' Ollie said. 'As long as my hair looks OK ...'

Alex had switched on the radio and Travie McCoy's 'Billionaire' was bursting through the sound system and we were all singing along loudly. One of our main fears was that we would be seen as arrogant and stuck-up because we liked to think of ourselves as pretty down-to-earth. We were just living our lives like many other twenty-something-year-olds in London. We worked hard during the day, went out almost every night and then had to deal with dreadful hangovers the next morning. Life was all about spontaneity, partying and having fun, and I lived from day to day, spending too much time dancing on tables in my favourite clubs and looking at the receipts in my wallet the next morning and wincing when I clocked the amount I had spent. I'm surprisingly generous when I'm drunk. And normally I've lost my phone, make-up case or another vital element from my bag at some point in the night, if it has been a big one.

We were just living our lives like many other twenty-something-year-olds in London

'What if we were to open a magazine and see our pictures staring back at us?' Cheska asked. 'How amazing would it be to be asked to take part in a photo shoot, where we get our hair and make-up done by a make-up artist and get to choose our clothes with a special stylist? That would be so much fun!'

While Ollie hoped his long locks would look shiny, my worries about being on camera were mainly about having to wash my hair more than once a week and coping with having to look immaculate all the time. I just wasn't that kind of Chelsea girl. For me, getting dressed up meant throwing on an oversized jumper over some leggings, running a brush through my hair and slapping on a bit of make-up. Getting ready took all of ten minutes. My other big concern was that I would come out with some seriously stupid things; my general knowledge and common sense were – and still are – somewhat lacking. The problem is that I tend to speak before really thinking about what I'm about to say!

More than anything, the idea that I would become well known seemed completely outrageous.

Fast-forward four years, and my life has changed beyond measure in such a fantastic way. Back when I started on *Made in Chelsea*, I was working as a receptionist for a hedge-fund company, but I was never cut out for a desk job, especially one in the finance world, where everyone was sitting behind their computers by 8.30 a.m. and worked hard for ten hours solid, regardless of whether they had been out the night before or not. I was late into the office almost every morning, because of staying out until the early hours, and never learnt much. Once I famously thought that Bloomberg, the financial software and data company that tracks the markets, was a type of flower. And on another occasion I was instructed to fetch celery for my bosses' Bloody Marys for the weekly Friday drinks and came back from the shop carrying a lettuce. I had no idea about what my future would look like, but I could never have imagined it the way it has turned out.

The impact of *Made in Chelsea* on my life was immediate. And while the positives are huge, and I still can't really take it in when I see myself in the likes of *Grazia* and *OK!*, it's not all been easy – something you'll read more about later.

The opportunities that have come my way have been amazing: things like winning a BAFTA, launching my own line of clothing with Lipstick Boutique and my own range of nail polishes called Binky London, as well as filming in far-flung destinations around the world and even writing my own *Daily Mail* beauty blog. These are what dreams are made of.

In this book, I hope to give you an insight into what life has been like for me, growing up in the idyllic countryside in a beautiful house, surrounded by animals and older siblings, my parents' subsequent sad divorce and my battle with bullies at one of the schools I attended shortly after their split. I will also take you behind the scenes and tell you all about my relationships, on and off the screen, and will give you all my best fashion, dating and Chelsea-girl tips. I really hope you enjoy reading it – make sure you let me know via Twitter @binkyfelstead. If you like it, Jägerbombs all round!

Binky x

> *In this book, I hope to give you an insight into what life has been like for me*

1

HOW MY *MADE IN CHELSEA* DREAM BEGAN

Made in Chelsea shows off everything I love about living in London. When I see the opening segments panning through montages of whitewashed Victorian villas, fast cars accelerating down the exclusive streets, incredible designer fashions, popping champagne corks and the background buzz in one of my favourite nightclubs on the King's Road, I have to pinch myself. In some ways it hasn't really sunk in how my life has changed, because everything has happened so quickly. While a lot of the cast were brought up in the more affluent parts of London like Mayfair and Chelsea and had incredibly privileged childhoods, I think I represent the other end of the – admittedly also very privileged – Chelsea spectrum: the down-to-earth, country-loving, dog-owning

Made in Chelsea shows off everything I love about living in London

1

tomboy, who only recently started to think about what I wore and began washing my hair more than once a week when I got one too many Tweets about how everyone loved the fact that I 'didn't give a shit'.

The whole *Made in Chelsea* journey started for me one night back in late 2010, when I was in a late-night bar called Barts on Sloane Avenue, watching a country-singer friend, who was performing a gig there. I was with my flatmate Cheska Hull and we were having a few drinks and a dance. I was probably living like a lot of other twenty-year-olds in London, working during the day and then going out almost every night until the early hours, enjoying the freedom and endless choice of bars and clubs in Chelsea and Fulham, and dragging myself out of bed with a banging headache the next day to go to work.

I was working as a receptionist for a company in Marylebone, and the two owners were really good to me. I was often late and used every reason under the sun as to why I wasn't at my desk when everyone else was. London Underground featured heavily in my list of excuses but some- times found myself saying things like 'my hamster died'. I think they knew it was simply the case that I pressed the snooze button on my alarm clock more than I should and that I had terrible hangovers! I have never been able to drink wine.

Cheska and I had met when I was looking for a flat to share in 2009, after I had been living in London for a year or so. A friend of mine knew of a room going free in a large house in Parsons Green, sharing with a trainee accountant called Kate and her brother and a PR girl whom everyone called Cheska. I knew the area quite well already, because I had been living with my mum there since leaving school. As soon as I met Cheska, with her big blonde hair, boy stories and bubbly personality, I knew we'd get on brilliantly. We clicked immediately and from that point we went out together a lot, either at house parties or clubbing. We had huge house parties at the flat with all our friends and went out almost every night. We would come back late at night and terrorise our other flat-

As soon as I met Cheska, with her big blonde hair, boy stories and bubbly personality, I knew we'd get on brilliantly

mate, whom we later nicknamed Square due to her email rants, telling us off about waking her up or stealing her clothes. We would jump on her bed at three o'clock in the morning and then run down the stairs and drink the champagne that she was saving for a special occasion. We were so naughty.

Barts is a smallish venue and it was quite dark inside. Listening to our friend performing some of his tracks, Cheska and I were chatting and dancing away when a young guy and girl came up to us and introduced themselves. They were really friendly and told us they were looking for people who lived in Chelsea and the surrounding areas to star in a new reality TV show. A few months previously, Cheska and I had starred in our very own episode of the MTV show *My Super Sweet World Class*. Cheska had been approached via her work in PR to organise a party for 300 people with a vintage-Hollywood theme and I had helped her and the episode was called *Cheska and Binky's Hollywood Party*. We had filmed solidly for a week, so by then we were used to having cameras pointing at us.

We went out with them and started telling them all about our families, relationships and sex lives. I knew that I would have to be totally myself. I imagine pretending to be someone else is pretty hard work, so I was completely true to how I am all the time. I didn't want to play games; I just wanted to have fun and make them laugh. The stories about my nights out gradually got more outrageous. 'So far, so good,' I thought to myself and started to feel more confident that I might make it onto the show. They giggled a lot as we recounted tales of drunken nights out and stupid games we played on each other. I hoped they liked us and would get in touch.

A few days after our encounter at Barts, I was contacted about the show. I felt a bit confused by it all and still didn't believe that it would go anywhere. I figured the best it could be was one of those one-series shows on an obscure satellite channel, but I was really excited about the possibility of starring in another TV show because after the initial nerves, I had loved filming for MTV. Deep down, as much as I liked my colleagues at work, I knew that corporate life wasn't for me and I was excited by the prospect of being on TV and taking a different path. I really wanted to make it.

A week or so later we met up with the team behind the show again. I don't remember anyone else being out that night, apart from Cheska and Ollie, whom I had been very friendly with for about a year. Ollie and I initially 'met' when a mutual friend tried to set me up on a date with him. I remember that when I checked out his profile picture on Facebook and spotted his long, shiny black locks, I thought, 'I am not dating someone who's got longer hair than me!' and I quickly told my matchmaking friend that I didn't want to go on the double-date she had been planning, and that was that.

However, our paths were destined to cross again, because a few months later, I had been asked to do some club promotion work and needed someone to help me learn the ropes. A friend put me in touch with a guy called Alex Brocket, who was living with Ollie at the time. We agreed to meet at a pub called the White Horse, which everyone calls 'the Sloaney Pony', on the Fulham Road. Cheska was already there when we arrived, and I met Alex, who introduced us both to Ollie. Ollie was a club promoter as well and he was working on the door of various clubs, including Whisky Mist in Mayfair. After a few drinks at the bar and a chat about club promotion and what it entailed, Alex – who I guessed had taken a liking to me – asked Cheska and me back to dinner at his house, and we accepted the invitation.

I loved Ollie immediately; he was so flamboyant and different, with his hair straighteners, make-up and tracksuit bottoms. From that first evening we spent in each other's company, I thought he could be bisexual – surely no straight guy uses more mascara and bronzer than most

I loved Ollie immediately; he was so flamboyant and different, with his hair straighteners, make-up and tracksuit bottoms

women? He was really funny and had me in fits of laughter with his strange flirting techniques, which included him trying to stick his finger up my nose!

Nothing ever happened with Alex, but Ollie and I became closer and closer, and he started to hang out with Cheska and me all the time. After work we would head to one of our houses before going out or if we were really partied out, we would stay in at one of our houses. He even gave us the nicknames Tranny 1 and Tranny 2, because apparently we took so long to get ready for a night out. He's one to talk …

For a while, he did think he fancied me. One night after work, the three of us were hanging out at our house with a bottle of wine and a Domino's pizza, and it was getting quite late. Cheska went upstairs because she had clocked that Ollie really liked me, so she wanted to give us some 'alone time'. It wasn't until years later that he told me that when he finally edged closer to me on the sofa – we were both really quite pissed at that point – he slowly eased his arm around me and moved in for the kill, and as he turned to me, I had fallen fast asleep against his chest and was dribbling! He likes to remind everyone that on one occasion I said I would've kissed him if I was awake, but we're such good friends that the idea of that seems quite crazy now.

I never had any doubts about being in the show. I just wanted to go for it and I couldn't wait to get started

I never had any doubts about being in the show. I just wanted to go for it and I couldn't wait to get started.

Need-to-know Chelsea facts

👑 Chelsea (*n.*) [chel-see] is defined as a fashionable residential district on the north bank of the River Thames, in the Royal Borough of Kensington and Chelsea.

👑 The area used to be really popular with hippy and rock 'n' roll crowds and was a cool hotspot for musicians like Bob Marley, the Beatles and the Rolling Stones. It was the epicentre of the Swinging Sixties. In the 1970s it was also the heart of the punk movement and was home to Vivienne Westwood's boutique, Sex.

👑 The King's Road is a real shopping mecca and as well as being home to many high street shops, the nearby Sloane Street is one of London's premier shopping destinations, housing boutiques, including Cartier, Dolce & Gabbana, Gucci, Jimmy Choo and Louis Vuitton.

👑 As well as the amazing shopping, Chelsea is home to some of London's biggest events and visitor attractions, including the Saatchi Gallery, the Natural History Museum and the Victoria & Albert Museum.

- ♛ Loads of celebs have homes or once owned a house here: Madonna reportedly has several homes on Belgravia Square, dubbed 'Madonna mansions', while Kylie Minogue, Robbie Williams and Hugh Grant also have properties in SW3. I long to be able to afford a house here one day!

- ♛ Famous films that have been shot in Chelsea include Woody Allen's *Match Point*, starring Scarlett Johansson and Jonathan Rhys Meyers; *Wimbledon* featuring Paul Bettany and Kirsten Dunst and the legendary *Clockwork Orange*, directed by Stanley Kubrick.

- ♛ The nightlife in Chelsea is incredible and there are countless exclusive bars, clubs and restaurants to visit. Most of the biggest and best clubs, like Raffles and Maggie's, are based on – or near to – the King's Road or Fulham Road.

2

MUDDY FIELDS AND NAKED BOTTOMS

I was never supposed to have been born. Mum is very open about the fact that I was a huge surprise to everyone, not least her. Dad was working hard with his business in information software, and Mum and Dad were travelling a lot around the world with his job. Mum was the perfect corporate wife, accompanying him on all his business trips. They had only just returned from the Middle East, where they had spent two years living in Bahrain with my older sister, Anna-Louise – whom we call AL – and my brother, Oliver. They relocated from London to Sussex and, with two children and their land full of animals – chickens, horses, dogs, cats: you name it, we had it – Mum and Dad decided that their little family was complete.

Mum is very open about the fact that I was a huge surprise to everyone, not least her

On a holiday in Barbados, Mum's contraception failed and not long after their return, she knew something was up, so, armed with a Clearblue pregnancy test, she hid in the downstairs loo. As the blue lines appeared, she said out loud, 'Shit, I'm pregnant,' and practically passed out from the shock. Mum kept the fact that she was expecting me totally secret for a day and a half, even lying to the dentist during a routine appointment, and when she eventually broke the news to my father, Roger, she said, 'I'm pregnant and I'm very happy about it, but it's really your decision too. What do we do about this?' Life was on the up for them and they had thought that the baby years, full of sleepless nights and dirty nappies, were well and truly over. Dad worked hard, but they had loads of expenses, like a big mortgage, holidays and school fees, and they enjoyed a great lifestyle, so me coming along really threw a spanner in the works. Mum was nervous about his reaction, but when she told him, he seemed pleased.

'Well, if you're happy to go with it, then I am too,' he told her. They hugged and laughed and that was it; I was here to stay.

Mum and Dad met at a party Mum was hosting at her parents' country club, Bonningtons, in the Hadhams, near Hunsdon in Hertfordshire. The year was 1978. My mum, Jane, was an only child and had a very privileged upbringing. As well as owning the country club, my mum's stepfather – whose name was Cliffy – had metal-spinning factories in London, invested in property and was hugely successful. Mum's real father died when she was just a year old, although it was never talked about when she was growing up. Cliffy became her dad, and she says he was everything she could've hoped for in a father and then some. She adored him.

My grandmother didn't come from such a wealthy family. She was born in the 1930s, in the East End of London. Her name was Honoria, but she hated it, so as soon as she could, when she was about fifteen, she changed it by deed poll. She wanted to be like the Beverley Sisters – a trio of pop-star sisters who were always in the music charts at the time – and called herself Babs, after one of them. Babs then became Ba Ba, or Ba, which was how I knew her. As soon as she was old enough, Ba Ba upped and left the East End and travelled hundreds of miles to work in a hotel in Norfolk.

It was in Norfolk that she met my grandfather, who was a gentleman farmer who owned land up in Lincolnshire. He was blown away by her beauty; it's such a romantic story. He was more than forty years older than her and would whisk Ba Ba off in his Bentley on exciting dates. Later, he sent her to Lucie Clayton's, which was a famous 'finishing' school in London, where she learnt hostessing skills like flower-arranging, cookery and deportment and how to be a 'lady'. I smile when I think of Ba Ba doing that kind of stuff, because she was always so spirited and fun and would always say it as it was. My mum was born when Ba Ba was just twenty-one.

Ba Ba moved back to London after the death of her first husband and was working in Holborn as a smart gentlemen's manicurist. Every barber worth his salt back then had a manicurist on the staff, and City gentlemen getting their nails done was very common. Cliffy strolled in one day and clocked Ba Ba looking petite and pretty in the corner. She took one of his soft hands in hers to inspect his nails, looked into his eyes and that was that.

When she was young, Ba Ba modelled knitwear and had the most spectacular boobs you could ever imagine; they were just immense. Her bras were enormous, like parachutes, and when we were kids, my brother Ollie and I would always marvel at their sheer size. We would put them over our heads and fit loads of stuff in them, like some sort of handbag, and howl with laughter. As a child, I remember Ba Ba being lovely, and she was one of life's cuddlers – she was always hugging us into her huge chest and smothering us. She was very protective, telling us that everything would be all right, and she called me 'darling'. People say I am the spitting image of her and I am really flattered by the comparison.

People say I am the spitting image of her and I am really flattered by the comparison

Ba Ba adored her animals and always had dogs at her home. Bonnington's Country Club had a huge stable yard at the back, and Ba Ba and Cliffy would take in stray dogs, which would be given to them by various people. If there was a dog that needed a home, Ba Ba would welcome it into the house, however scraggy, smelly or decrepit it was, and lovingly nurse it back to health. When Mum and Dad met, there were eleven dogs there that had been rescued, and Mum had six of her own to add to the tally. Ba Ba would take her dogs around, like a pack of children of all different shapes and sizes, in the back of her Range Rover and when she opened the door, they would all spill out. She never minded adding a few more to her clan. When Mum was heavily pregnant with AL, she had two springer spaniels called Ollie and Danny, which Cliffy had given her the money to buy, but they got a skin disease called mange and Mum found it hard to cope, so Ba Ba took them in and spent an entire weekend bathing them for her in her own bathroom. Nothing was too much trouble when it came to her animals. The only thing that would ever make Ba Ba angry with us when we were children was when she found that we hadn't given the dogs fresh water or were late feeding them.

My mum was brought up in London and went to a convent school in Hampstead. She had a very unconventional upbringing and for a long time she hated the fact that her parents weren't like those of her school friends or the other children she saw living nearby. Ba Ba and Cliffy didn't consider education as particularly important, so schoolwork, 'A' grades and exams just weren't high on their list of priorities. Ba Ba stuck close to Cliffy and often went to his workplace just to be with him, and Mum would beg Ba Ba to pick her up from school like ordinary mums, which she rarely did. She also longed for Ba Ba to swap her stilettos for a pair of altogether more sensible brogues, like the ones her friends' mothers wore. On one occasion they went on holiday and the weather was terrible but Ba Ba completely failed to pack anything for Mum in the way of practical clothing. All she had with her were some pretty dresses and sparkly shoes. It would never have occurred to Ba Ba to have bought Mum anything along the lines of an anorak or woolly jumper because she thought they were ugly.

Most nights, after Mum had come home from school, Ba Ba and Cliffy would head off in their big black Cadillac – they always had big American saloon cars – and go clubbing, or to smart restaurants and exclusive launch parties. They were quite flash and enjoyed a very glamorous lifestyle full of champagne, designer dresses and nights out at the best restaurants, bars and hotels in the capital. On some occasions, when Mum was still young, they would send a car for her in the middle of the night and she would go out with them.

They were quite flash and enjoyed a very glamorous lifestyle full of champagne, designer dresses and nights out at the best restaurants, bars and hotels in the capital

One time, when she was only around eight years old, Cliffy called home in the early hours and Mum was fast asleep in bed. The phone woke Mum up and Cliffy told her he was sending a black cab to pick her up from home so she could join them at the opening night of the Hilton Hotel on Park Lane. She put on one of her best flouncy party dresses, of which she had many, and hopped into the car. As she drew up to the hotel, Cliffy was waiting for her outside, dressed in his smart top hat and evening suit, with a black-and-white silk tie. He scooped her up and took her inside, where the three of them spent the night dancing away together. That night Cliffy and Mum won the competition for the oldest and youngest people on the dance floor. Mum still has loads of pictures of herself at nightclubs when she was really very young, posing and smiling alongside all sorts of famous people. Even when Mum was a child, Ba Ba used to say to her, 'You're much more sensible than me. You're the adult.' Mum pretty much brought herself up, and has lived like that ever since – by the seat of her pants!

Ba Ba refused to change her fun and eccentric ways as she grew older. One day, when she went to pick up AL from school, she turned up in a pair of black sixteen-hole Doc Marten boots. When AL had grown up and was working as an artist, she started exhibiting her art professionally and would often host private views, and we would all go along and support her. On one occasion Ba Ba turned up a bit tipsy to one of her exhibitions, after popping a champagne cork on the train on the way to London and drinking the entire bottle herself.

My dad's upbringing was very different to Mum's – more middle class and sedate. He grew up in Cuffley in Hertfordshire and attended a grammar school there. He was fairly studious and loved playing the bass guitar and used to be in a band when he was younger. Dad's father, Richard – my granddad – used to be in the merchant navy and fought in the war and always had loads of great stories for us when we were children about the foreign adventures he'd had during his younger years. When Mum and Dad met, Granddad was working for the finance department of Bejam, a frozen food retailer, and my nana couldn't have been more different to Ba Ba if she tried.

Nana, whose name was Eileen, was a pillar of the community and used to do the church flowers and bake cakes. Both her and Granddad were into their gardening and Granddad worked so hard in their garden that his hands were rough, like sandpaper. Their house was spotless and like some sort of show home, so when I stayed, I was always nervous about making a mess. Dad also had a younger sister, Jill, and I got the impression that he was seen as a bit of a rebel in his family. When we were growing up we spent some great Christmases with our cousins on that side of the family, Laura, Mark and Beth.

So, back to the story of how Mum and Dad met. The party had a 'vicars and tarts' theme. Apparently Dad was with a redhead who had just been awarded the prize for the best tart, but she hadn't actually dressed up, she just looked naturally tarty. As Mum and Dad clapped eyes on each other, suddenly this crazy red-haired woman appeared from behind him and started yelling expletives at everyone and he scarpered as quickly as possible, to avoid causing any more of a scene. Mum, who was twenty-four at the time, had just come out of a marriage to a man called Roger, which had lasted for just six weeks, and when she saw Roger Mark II, it was love at first sight. He called the next day to apologise for the behaviour of his crazy companion – assuring Mum that that short-lived romance was most definitely off – and asked her out. The rest, as they say, is history.

They tied the knot at the Chelsea Register Office in 1978. I have the picture of them sitting alongside one another signing the wedding register, looking ridiculously young and gorgeous, in my house in Fulham. It was her second wedding at the Chelsea Register Office, because she had also married Roger Mark I there, and Ba Ba always said that while she liked the second wedding the best, she preferred the party after the first wedding because it was more fun! My older sister, AL, was a honeymoon baby and was born ten months later, in July 1979.

We have a thing for nicknames in my family. AL was very enthusiastic and serious as a child, with her white socks pulled up to her knees and her hair always beautifully neat and tidy. When she was at school, when all of the other kids were messing about and not concentrating, she would get so annoyed with them. On one occasion, all of her class were in the annual Christmas play and were lined up on stage singing 'We Wish You a Merry Christmas', but they weren't doing it quite to her liking and she took it upon herself to instruct this group of four-year-olds, saying very sternly, while wagging her finger, 'No, no, it's FIGGY pudding.' So she became Figgy. When Oliver came along in 1981, AL could only say 'Oliber', so he became Bear.

Apparently Mum's pregnancy with me was very difficult and it was a bit hit and miss for a while as to whether I would survive. She was instructed by Ba Ba to spend a lot of time lying down flat on her bed, resting, with her feet up in the air flat against the wall. Ba Ba would kill anyone who tried to come near Mum; she was so protective, especially because Dad wasn't around that much as he was working all the time. She would drive Mum to the hospital and she paid for all her private treatment without a second thought. I think it was quite an emotional time for everyone, because the experts said they didn't think the pregnancy would last.

I was born on 14th June 1990 at the Portland Hospital in London. Mum and Dad decided to call me Alexandra Elizabeth, because Mum loved the name Alexandra and all the girls in my family have Elizabeth as their middle name. Apparently, unlike my siblings, I was quite a cute newborn, with some brown hair and a pretty, straight nose. According to Mum, the midwife, Nuala, took me around the hospital corridors and showed me off to everyone who walked past. Maybe I was destined to be an exhibitionist from the first day!

My arrival caused mixed responses from Ollie and AL, who were aged nine and ten at the time. Mum had broken the news to AL, while Dad had told Ollie at the same time, and Dad had clearly done a better job by sandwiching the pregnancy news in the middle of talking about getting more chickens and buying a boat for the summers.

From the very start, my big brother was my idol. When I was a baby, Ollie would come from outside, where he had been feeding the chickens and ducks, and get my bottle from the fridge to feed me. His hands and nails would be caked with chicken and duck poo and he would be fiddling with the bottle teat, and it would be in my mouth and I would be drinking the milk before my mum could stop him. When I started to toddle around, I followed Ollie everywhere, like his shadow. He was funny, good-looking and strong, and taught me loads of practical skills, like how to ride a bike and how to play tennis and deliver a mean backhand. We were like two peas in a pod.

The nickname Binky was decided on early on. It was a combination of 'bad baby' and 'dinky', because I was so naughty. Perhaps having two older siblings made me stand up for myself more because I never did as I was told and always ques-

18

tioned everything. Mum and Dad would say yes, and I would say no. Ollie and I would play-fight all the time and he would rugby-tackle me, but I always tried to give as good as I got, so I was pretty tough too. My family always called me Binky from when I was tiny, but as a child I was Ali to my friends and at school. Later, when I moved to London, I changed from Ali to Alex, but when I met Cheska, she started calling me Binky as well. So she introduced me to everyone as Binky, and it has stuck.

I am a real countryside girl. I grew up in a huge flint home called Endlewick House, in the picturesque village of Arlington in East Sussex. The house was really old and homely, with ancient wooden beams, open fires and an old Aga in the kitchen, where there was always something cooking. At the back of the house there was a yard with four stables where we kept our horses and ponies, a tack room for storing the saddles, bridles and brushes and two massive muddy fields. We also had a large garden where we would play, with a pond at the end. There were all different types of animals, everywhere you looked.

Mum was mad about the horses. She had always ridden in Hyde Park and on holidays as a child and when she was a teenager she, Ba Ba and Cliffy moved away from London to a huge house in Kent. Around the time of the move, it was Christmas and they bought her first pony, and from then on she always had horses. I also started young; when I was just six months old, Mum dressed me in my warm pink snowsuit and put me on my sister's gentle pony, who was called Megan, in a special basket saddle so I didn't fall off. From then on, horses became my passion too.

As a toddler, I used to love being completely naked and would often be outside in the back garden with no clothes on, just wearing my favourite red wellies. A local farmer gave Mum a tractor tyre for me to play with. She put it in the garden and filled it with sand, and it was my very own giant sandpit. I would spend hours in there. I also loved helping out by feeding the baby goats and lambs and there are pictures of me feeding them with huge bottles of milk almost as big as my head, and I'm completely starkers.

We always had dogs – Harry and Harvey Nichols were golden retrievers and Tatiana, a Westie, was my dog – and we also had two cats, called Spagic and Minky. There were also rabbits and hamsters in hutches. I was always given a few small jobs to help out with the animals and, when he was at school, my brother used to breed ducks and chickens. In the morning, I would go outside to the pen they were in and pick up all the eggs that had been laid overnight, to help him. A few of the ducks were quite aggressive and there was one goose in particular that would always come after me and peck the back of my wellies. I would be screaming and running away and Mum would be chasing after it with the broom handle, trying to get it away from me. It was horrible and was always hanging around outside, and some days I didn't want to step outside the door in case the evil goose got me!

When I was tiny, apparently, I used to love whisky. I would sit in Dad's arms at the local pub, the Yew Tree, while Dad had a drink on a Saturday with his friends, which is what all the guys who lived nearby did to unwind after a busy week in the office. Dad was quite a big drinker, as were most of his friends.

Apparently, in the pub, I would be looking around with a glum face. I would then reach my little hand out and drag his glass towards me and put it to my mouth. Dad and all his friends would laugh, presuming that I would hate the taste of it, but it turned out that I loved it – and they had to wrench the glass away from me! On one occasion, after an afternoon at the bar and one too many drinks, Dad left me in the pub by mistake. I was happily sat in a highchair, gurgling away, and it was only when he got home and Mum asked him where I was that he remembered, and he said, 'Oh shit' and confessed. It wasn't a problem because we knew everyone at the pub, and when they went back to get me, I was happy as anything, being entertained by the regulars.

When I was still very young, Mum noticed that I had a learning difficulty. While my speech was normal – in fact, I wouldn't stop talking – she realised that I didn't seem to remember things in the way I should for my age and I wasn't keeping up with the children at the little school I had started at, called St Bede's. She couldn't help but compare my development to what AL and Ollie were doing when they were my age and also noticed that while all my little friends had their books with them when they came home to do homework, I didn't. The school claimed there was nothing wrong with my schoolwork and they had 'nothing but good things to say', but Mum was worried and took me out of St Bede's. I started at Dallington School, where there were loads of really bright children, and the teachers realised immediately there was a problem and referred Mum to a specialist to get more expert help.

In the end, we went to see a lady at Guy's Hospital in London who confirmed that I had an auditory memory problem, which meant I couldn't recall things as easily as other children. We ended up going to another specialist on Harley Street in London twice a week for about six months, where I did exercises like picture games, where I looked at items on a tray and then they were taken away and I tried to remember them. We also used to do stuff at home and Mum used to say to me, 'Get an apple, a pear and a carrot from around the kitchen,' but I would normally only remember one or two of the items. It was a minor thing and the sessions seemed to kick-start the right part of my brain and I was fine, but I never really enjoyed learning.

From Dallington School, I went to a prep school in Sussex called St Andrew's. The uniform was a grey pleated skirt, pull-up grey socks, a maroon jumper and a maroon-and-white striped shirt. In the summer we wore pretty summer dresses with white belts. I liked the uniform, but I hated school. I was always in the bottom set for everything and, looking back, I didn't process anything from my lessons. The only thing I remember learning about was the plague, in my history classes; everything else has gone from my memory, quite literally as if it went in one ear and straight out the other. I liked art and drama and I had singing lessons, which I enjoyed. I just don't feel I was cut out for learning like most people are, and I hated exams. I had to have

I just don't feel I was cut out for learning like most people are, and I hated exams

things explained to me in many different ways before any facts really sunk in. I found it much easier to understand concepts through pictures. I loved art because I was told I was good at it and I enjoyed experimenting with lots of different materials. It also didn't feel like learning, so was quite fun. Maths was the worst; I just didn't get it – for me, looking at numbers on a page is like looking at text in a foreign language. I still haven't got my maths GCSE and struggle even with simple sums.

I wasn't clever, so I was never particularly popular with the other children at my school. My best friend is called Letty and our parents were friends before we were even born. Her mum and dad, Louise and Rick, had a farm up the road and, like me, she loved horses and animals. She has long blonde hair and was incredibly sporty, fun and popular. While we both struggled at the beginning of our time at St Andrew's school, she quickly overtook me academically and made other friends and had her own posse to hang out with for a while. So school was not much fun really. I would count down the hours every day before the bell went and I would be picked up and could go home to be with my animals and my brother. Home was my own little heaven. It is still my favourite place in the world, and Ollie and I talk about buying the house back in the future.

We were a really sociable family and Mum and Dad had an open-house policy, where there were always people popping in for drinks, food and some company. My brother and sister would have their friends round all the time and they often stayed overnight. My brother's friends were all beautiful, so there was always a stream of good-looking boys trailing in and out of the house. All my friends from school adored my brother and thought he was the most handsome boy they had ever seen. He coached younger children in tennis at a sports club nearby and also snowboarded in the winter, which everyone thought was really cool. When I was seven and he was sixteen, he would have these huge house parties for all his friends at home. There was normally plenty of alcohol and girls there. Mum and Dad were really relaxed and, as a result, my brother, sister and I were all very open with them. Ollie's bedroom was next to mine and I used to pretend to be asleep and these boys used to come in one by one, a bit the worse for wear, and pass out on my floor, because they wanted to take a quick breather from the action. I used to watch them and think, 'All right. Anyone else coming in?'

Like most young girls, I loved my Barbie dolls. I had every Barbie under the sun and all the accompanying stuff, so my Barbies had their own houses, cars, furniture, horses and horseboxes. I used to spend hours in my room playing with them and would retreat into my own little world, making up stories about them. I liked to create my own little Barbie families, with Mummy, Daddy and baby Barbies. My brother and his friends used to listen outside the door and would take the piss out of me. When I left my bedroom to go to school or outside, he would come in and work his special Ollie magic. As a family, we were quite open about sex and I knew about the birds and bees from a very early age. I would come back and these Barbies would be in the most

As a family, we were quite open about sex

horrific sexual positions. Every Barbie would be with the wrong husband and even the kids were involved. They were bent over cars, in the car, in the horsebox, all at it, and I would be like, 'I can't play with them again. They're all with the wrong husbands!'

Mum and Dad used to host these amazing lavish drinks and dinner parties for their friends and it was a case of 'being seen and not heard' and then going to bed – or at least upstairs to our rooms – before they sat down for dinner and got drunk. I remember that, in the morning, I used to purposely wake up really early, while everyone else was still in bed, because all the drinks and chocolates would be left out on the table. It was an old house with creaky floorboards and I knew every creak in every wooden stair. I would creep downstairs as carefully and slowly as I could, like some sort of ninja, without making any noise. It would take me ages because I would have to go past Mum and Dad's bedroom and if Dad heard he would be really cross. More often than not, I succeeded in my mission and made it down without waking anyone up and, once downstairs, I would head to the dining room and gorge on the chocolates and remnants of the night before. Being in my childhood home was the happiest time I can remember.

My top Chelsea-girl hostess tips

Mum and Dad hosted lots of wonderful parties while I was growing up in Sussex and I love having people over to my house for parties and supper. Here are my top ten tips to make sure things go off without a hitch.

♕ Use trusted recipes and make food ahead of time. If you are hosting dinner for friends or just serving canapés with your drinks, make sure you make the food beforehand. Practise one weekend, then dish the food up the following week. I like homely treats like pigs in blankets and smoked salmon blinis.

♕ Prepare the scene. Light some candles and scatter them around the room and put flowers on the table to create a homely atmosphere. Before the party, set out as much food as possible, so you don't have to go back and forth to the kitchen when your guests arrive. Or, if it's a dinner party, do as much as you can beforehand, so you only have to do last-minute things during your party.

♕ Greet the guests. Make sure you have enough time to make yourself look glam and meet all your guests at the door. Introduce people to one another if they haven't met before – and, as you do, throw in an interesting piece of information about them to get the conversation going.

Keep invites simple. For formal events, like twenty-first birthday parties or weddings, I think it is good to send sophisticated card invites in the post because it always makes the event stand out and seem really special. For more informal gatherings, sending invites via Facebook is much easier, but make sure you put 'invite only', so no strangers turn up and people don't bring loads of friends with them. Double-check your list to make sure you haven't inadvertently missed anyone off the all-important list.

 Have enough booze. Every good party needs lots of alcohol, so make sure you have a few bottles of red wine and a few bottles of white, so your guests can choose what they would like. I always like to kick drinks off with a glass of champagne or a cocktail. I don't think you can go too wrong with some bubbles!

 Plan the seating. If you're having a dinner party, make a proper seating plan. It's traditional to sit married couples apart, but engaged couples and those who are dating together. I always like being among my friends, although being mixed up can be a great way to meet new people and I have had loads of brilliant nights meeting people for the first time and getting drunk together.

Keep control. If things get out of hand and more people turn up than you originally expected, kick out anyone who is making trouble and after that I advise that you just have a few more drinks to try to relax. Leave the clean-up job for the next day and make sure you drink a few glasses of water before going to bed.

 Dress code. It's sometimes fun to state a dress code for your party. Fancy dress or a themed dress code, like neon, can be great, and black-tie is always an easy option if you're stuck for ideas. Make sure you look fabulous; you are the hostess after all!

 Relax and enjoy yourself. It's very easy when you are hosting a party to not have fun yourself because you are making sure everyone else is happy. Don't worry about the mess, leave the dishes until the next day and relax.

 Have a cool playlist. Everyone loves the music on my iPod and I always have the best party playlists. I love lots of different kinds of music, from old-school artists like Dire Straits, Phil Collins and Bon Jovi, through to house and electric. It's a pretty eclectic mix, but people always like my music.

3

THE FELLIES' HAPPY HOLIDAYS

As well as a happy home life, we had great family holidays a couple of times a year; we were so fortunate. In the winter we went skiing in places like Chamonix, Val d'Isère, Verbier and Belle Plagne in the French Alps.

There was a group of families nearby that clubbed together and raised money for a local boy, Charlie Boutwood, whom I played with and who had a rare brain tumour. He was at Great Ormond Street for about a year and a half and the family needed money to send him to a special healer. The charity fund was called Charlie's Challenge and the local families, including mine, would organise massive dinner-dances at places like the Grand Hotel in Brighton, where they

In the winter we went skiing in places like Chamonix, Val d'Isère, Verbier and Belle Plagne in the French Alps

29

would donate gifts to be auctioned and bid on other things.

For a few years Charlie's father organised an annual trip where all the families would go down to Belle Plagne in the French Alps; we all stayed in the same hotel and had a great time together. They called it 'Boutwood Bound'. We would always drive over because we had so much luggage and all our ski gear. It was so exciting because Mum would wake us up at the crack of dawn and my parents would pack up the Range Rover to the hilt and we would drive to Dover, where we would get the ferry over to Calais and continue on from there along the French motorways towards the Alps. Dad would be in the driving seat with Mum next to him and, as the youngest, I would be in the back, sandwiched between AL and Ollie. Ollie was always particularly grumpy after being woken up early so would have his earphones in, ignoring everyone. We would have duvets and pillows in the back with us, so it was really cosy and we could sleep if we wanted to. Mum would turn on Bryan Adams and Sting full volume as we sped down the motorways, and we would all sing along. It was a great bonding time for us. By the time we got near the resort, it was always late at night and we would have to drive up the winding mountain path to the hotel. I remember it being pitch-black and icy. I would look over the edge of the snowy mountain and feel a bit freaked out. My brother would helpfully tell me that we were going to roll off the edge!

We would spend the days whizzing up and down the slopes – I was never scared; I was a real daredevil and would just go for it. Mum and Dad always sent me to ski school in the mornings, so they could go off and have some grown-up time together. I hated it, because I didn't know anyone or understand the language. My mum would pack me off in the morning with some KitKats and a drink in my bumbag and I would be dragged kicking and screaming to the ski school, although, about five minutes later, I would forget what the fuss was all about. When we moved up a class, we were given these special metal snowflakes. The fact that I didn't understand the language would unnerve me, and for a few years, when I was really little, I remember being too scared to ask the ski instructor if I could go to the loo, so would just wee inside my snowsuit.

In the afternoons we would all ski together, and we have loads of videos in a box somewhere of all our trips. We took the family camcorder everywhere. Dad was always in charge, which we hated because he used to go round trying to do atmospheric shots of the mountainside, like David Attenborough. From time to time, my brother would take the camera off him and would stick it down his trousers to record his willy or ski off down the mountain with it at breakneck speed, while Dad shouted, 'Slow, go slow. Why are you going so quick, Oliver? Stop it! SLLLOWWW!'

After we'd packed up our skis for the day, had hot showers and changed and eaten supper at the hotel restaurant, there was fun stuff to do with the other children, like singing karaoke or doing pub-style quizzes. We danced at the hotel disco and I practised the moves that AL had taught me. After that, we would just run around the hotel. I was always with loads of the older kids and I remember my brother trying to give me my first cigarette for a joke, to show off to the others. I was probably only about seven. I always did what he told me to, so when we were standing outside the hotel and he said, 'Have some of this,' passing me a lit cigarette, as everyone gathered round to watch and laugh. I remember taking it off him carefully, putting it to my mouth and slowly inhaling, then coughing up my guts and feeling really sick and light-headed. I thought I would never ever touch a cigarette again after that.

The hotel bill at the end of the holiday was always an issue because we would order loads of food and drinks and just put it on Dad's tab. My brother was the worst culprit. We would start sucking up to Dad on the last morning of the holiday, in preparation for when he clapped eyes on the bill and almost fainted. Looking back, we were so spoiled and carefree and, understandably, Dad would be so cross with us. The drive home tended to be a far quieter affair because Dad was in such a bad mood.

Every year we went to a place called Rock on the Cornish coast for a week or so in August. It was a real family tradition. We stayed at the Old Customs House, which was opposite a restaurant and bar called the Mariners that everyone used to go to. I was a bit young to appreciate it, but I loved the buzz of having lots of people around me. There was a sea of famil-iar faces spilling over the pavements and road outside.

Rock is nicknamed 'Chelsea on Sea' and there were always loads of families from Chelsea and Sussex that we knew having a holiday, too. My brother and sister went out drinking with their friends and had the best time going to beach parties and barbecues. During the days, we would have picnics on the beach or take a trip on the boat or go to Polzeath or Port Isaac, and the nights would involve plenty of booze. The area featured in a Channel 4 show called *Posh Rock*, back in 2000, where Mum and Dad talked about the crazy party atmosphere. It was my first run-in with the TV cameras and you can see me getting one of the dogs out of the back of the Range Rover. Blink and you'll miss me!

For a week every summer, I also used to go to Pony Club camp with my grey Connemara pony, Callie. Mum used to do showing events with AL, where she would mount a beautifully turned-out pony just outside the ring and go and do her thing, hopefully being placed in the top three, before coming out again and dismounting. Mum wanted me to be more involved in every aspect of horses and, as a result, I used to be in my element mucking out and getting my hands dirty. We would often travel halfway across the country to go and look at ponies to buy – and we always chose really good ones, with bags of personality and loads of talent. I helped Mum to feed them every morning and turned them out into the fields with the right rugs on, groomed and rode them, although Mum claims it was under sufferance!

The annual Pony Club camps were held at a few different locations, but we had our own little dormitories and the most important thing would be whom we were sharing with because there were loads of kids there that we didn't know. When we arrived we would race towards the list of names, squealing. I would always be sharing with Letty and Fleur, another girl whom I grew up with. Mum would let me take this massive bag of sweets because Letty's mum would never let her have any, so I would sneak them in and share them around until we all felt sick from the sugar rush. At night we would gather round in our sleeping bags and tell each other ghost stories with torches shining on our faces and freak each other out. We would have two hour-long horse-riding lessons each day and maybe a talk about some aspect of horse care and we would spend hours grooming our ponies until they shone. There were silly competitions like who had kept the best stable and who had the cleanest tack. At the end of the week all the parents would be invited along and trophies would be given out. Mum often rocked up midway through the week with a cake or some biscuits she had made and I always loved seeing her.

I had a great riding teacher called Deborah Barr who taught me how to be a better rider by putting me on all her naughty ponies. They would play up but, because I was so strong, I was never scared. Sometimes she would put me on ponies that were like bucking broncos, but if I fell off, I would stand up, brush myself down and get straight back on and – touch wood – I've never had any bad injuries, like broken bones, only the odd black and blue bruise. I was made to wear a body protector, which are like hard foam suits that protect your spine and back if you fall off or are kicked. They aren't particularly fashionable, so I felt like a bit of a loser wearing one, but they clearly worked. I loved jumping lessons and would go over a jump and then round the arena and Deborah would raise the jump up by two holes each time, until it was level with my pony's head. We used to call it 'jumping the washing machine' because it was so high. I remember thinking, 'How will I ever survive this?' and then shutting my eyes and going for it, and the thrill of actually getting over the jump was incredible. It felt like flying. I have always found that riding is the one thing that really clears my head.

AL and I are very different, but when I was little, she used to do things like patiently teach me the dance moves to the Macarena. Mum tells me that as a child I was a 'diamond on the dance floor' and that I have AL to thank for that. AL has always been super-bright and seriously arty and she now works as an artist in New York. She used to dress me up in weird stuff and put me in strange poses so she could paint or draw me for one of her GCSE and A-Level art projects. She was also hugely practical and very grown-up, so she would often help to entertain me if Mum was busy. As a child, I used to knacker Mum out because I was so naughty and never did what I was told. Apparently I got away with a lot more than AL and Ollie did when they were younger and I was very annoying in their eyes.

When I had the long holidays in the summer, and Mum used to despair about what she was going to do to keep me busy every day for eight long weeks, AL used to write very detailed timetables for her, with hourly slots for what I would be doing and where. She would also always help me with my homework, which I struggled with. One summer holiday I was supposed to have written a diary every day about what I had been doing, and suddenly the moment came when I was going back to school a few days later and

I hadn't written a single word, so AL did it all for me without complaint.

When I got slightly older, AL would take me shopping for clothes, and she came with me to get my ears pierced when I was about twelve one day after school in Eastbourne. She is so precise, she didn't like the spot of antiseptic that the beautician had marked on my ear, so she spat on her finger and rubbed the mark off, so I then got an ear infection.

She was a great source of information when it came to periods and girly stuff like that

She also took me to my first ever bra-fitting that year – and took pictures to send to her friends, which was embarrassing. She was a great source of information when it came to periods and girly stuff like that, when I didn't want to ask Mum.

I wasn't really scared of anyone or anything. Dad and I would often clash because he thought he automatically deserved respect from me, because that was how he had been brought up, but I would challenge him and talk back to him. We first fell out properly when I was seven years old and, from then on, it wasn't an easy relationship. When he said no, I would always ask why and then do whatever it was anyway. I remember one holiday in particular, when it was just Mum, Dad and I in a luxury resort, but there was nothing much to do. I was really bored and, as a result, behaved like a bit of a brat. Dad and I spent the entire time arguing, which probably spoiled the holiday for everyone.

Looking back on the situation now, I'm glad I was put in my place because I was quite cheeky and I think these days lots of kids get away with murder, so I'm happy I was disciplined. I took lots of things, like wonderful holidays and my ponies, for granted. I know I would be a nightmare now if I hadn't been told off, and I think I will be the same when I have kids. It's really important to have boundaries and discipline.

I'm glad I was put in my place because I was quite cheeky and I think these days lots of kids get away with murder

I don't think Mum and Dad's relationship was that happy and, as I got older, I realised that they never spent much time together, unless they were with their friends or with AL, Ollie and I. Sometimes I would hear them arguing or slamming doors at night, when they thought I was asleep.

Dad was too frantically busy to be involved in day-to-day family life. He adored his job in the City. In one of his workplaces they even had a bar that they'd open every evening after work, and on Fridays they would drink late into the evening, so he was never really at home during the week that much. As a result of that, he wasn't involved in the things that AL, Ollie and I were doing, and horses weren't an interest of his but were my huge love. I didn't really mind him not being around. Looking back, I can see he did his best, but it was a difficult relationship.

As youngsters, my relationship with my brother never wavered, despite the nine-year age gap. We were as thick as thieves and would often gang up against AL. We used to steal all of her sweets and tease her mercilessly. I wasn't immune to the pranks either; Ollie would often wind me up, and I was really gullible and never seemed to learn. Mum and Dad would often need to go away overnight for work and, by the time he was sixteen or seventeen and I was seven or eight, they would leave me in his capable hands, which, looking back, is a bit of a terrifying thought. One night, when Mum and Dad were away, he came into my bedroom and spotted a huge jar of sweets that Dad had given me after he had been away on a work trip. Clearly wanting his fair share, he waited until my parents were long gone and it was completely dark outside. He came running into my room, where I was playing with my Barbies.

'Ah, there are three really ugly witches outside your bedroom door!' he said.

'What? Really?'

'Yes, really, Binks. Quick, hide under your bed or they'll get you.'

I scurried under my bed as quickly as I could.

'Do you know what will make the witches go away?' he asked.

'No, what?' I asked, wide-eyed and terrified.

'If we eat all the sweets. But we have to eat all of them. Every last one.'

'Ah, OK then! Quick, have some,' I said, handing him a massive handful.

We spent about three hours eating them and each time I threatened to come out from under the bed, he would say, 'But, Binks, the witches are still out there. They'll get you,' which made me scream and dash back under the bed, while he smirked, with his cheeks bursting with sweets. I believed everything he said and hung on to his every word.

Another time, Mum and Dad were away overnight, leaving me in the capable hands of my brother once again. By then, AL had done her art foundation course in Brighton and gone on to St Martin's College in London, so it was just the two of us left at the family home. Ollie picked me up from school in my sister's new car. We'd been invited to a family friend's house for dinner because they knew Mum and Dad were away. They had a lovely home, which had big metal gates operated by a sensor and, as we left, like a boy racer, Ollie drove too fast over the gate sensors and broke the engine. A couple of miles down the road, he thought it would be funny to take a diversion to Michelham Priory, which is famous in the area for being haunted by various troubled ghosts. Just as we got near the long gravel driveway, the engine spluttered and the car drew to a slow and painful halt. It must've been about 11 p.m. and it was pitch-black outside and there was a thick mist drifting past the window. We couldn't see a thing. It was like something out of a horror film.

'Right, Binks, I'm gonna go and find a phone,' he said, and left me in the car, screaming, expecting to the see the famous grey lady or the black-hooded monk. I was absolutely petrified; I don't think I've ever been so scared. Eventually, he managed to make contact with our friends, who towed us home, but if we thought the spooky events were over for the night, we were wrong. In the early hours of the morning, I was woken up by Ollie shaking me, looking terrified. There was this awful noise of doors slamming and banging and we were convinced there was somebody, or something, in the house with us. Ollie got a poker from the fireplace and was yelping, 'Binky, can you come into my bed? I'm scared.' He then rang his best friend, whom he called Coxy, telling him he thought there was something in the house. Eventually, he plucked up the courage to go downstairs, still clutching the poker, and, far from being an awful ghost, it turned out that one of our dogs had got his head stuck between two doors and was trying to get it out!

I remember Christmas at Endlewick House as being a really magical time every year. Mum, who is the perfect homemaker, would decorate the house to within an inch of its life. The tree would be huge and dripping with tasteful decorations, like it had come straight out of a *Grazia* or *Tatler* shoot. There would be holly strung up everywhere and a beautiful festive wreath hanging on the front door. The stairs had ribbon woven down through the banisters and a big colourful stocking at the end, exploding with pretend presents. I remember putting red ribbons around clementines and sticking cloves into them with AL, so the house always smelt amazing. There would always be something delicious cooking in the bottom of the Aga and old-school Christmas tunes playing through the sound system. The fire would be crackling and the house was always warm and cosy. On all the surfaces, there would be Christmas cards. We always sent lots of Christmas cards and it is a tradition we still have – it's something that I hope will never die. I love receiving them.

One of our most magical Christmas traditions revolved around the Christmas fairy, which sat on top of the tree every year. Before I was born, when Mum and Dad were in Bahrain and Christmas was pretty much non-existent until the day before, she made a fairy by hand and every year it would go on top of our Christmas tree. When Christmas was over and Mum took down the decorations, she would tell me that the fairy had flown away, and the next Christmas, when we were decorating the house, she would tell me that the fairy will be flying back to us. Mum would say, 'I wonder when the fairy is going to arrive? I wonder where she's going to be?'

I would search high and low around the house for the fairy and, as Christmas approached, we would be eating breakfast and Mum would say, 'I have a feeling the fairy might arrive today.'

'Really, really?' I would reply and run around looking for her. She would be on the sofa, standing on the stairs or sitting on the mantelpiece and I would shout, 'Mummy, Mummy, she's arrived!' I would be bursting with excitement because I genuinely believed she had flown back just in time for Christmas. I can't wait to do the same for my kids when I'm older. It was the best tradition.

I also believed in the tooth fairy, although I hated it when my baby teeth fell out. Like most people, I hate going to the dentist. Just the very thought of those baby teeth hanging by a string would make me shudder and losing them was often a long and drawn-out process. Ollie used to jokingly threaten to tie my wobbly tooth to the doorknob and slam the door shut. Often, in the end, Mum would have to take a tissue and yank them out for me. I almost still believe in the magic of the tooth fairy because, one night, I put my old tooth under my pillow and prayed in my head for a Fruit Pastille and a diamond, rather than the one-pound coin the fairy normally gave me for each tooth. I woke up the next morning and, when I lifted up my pillow, there was an orange Fruit Pastille and a plastic diamond lying there. A few years later, I told my brother about it and he told me he'd put the sweet there, along with a plastic diamond he'd removed from one of AL's earrings. My brother says he overheard me, which I don't believe, because I remember praying in my head and not speaking out loud!

On Christmas Eve I would put out a mince pie and a glass of sherry for Father Christmas and a carrot for the reindeers on the mantelpiece above the fire, and in the morning I would come down the stairs bursting with anticipation. There was always an empty glass and the mince pie would have a bite taken out of it and the carrot would be gone. The whole family managed to keep the Father Christmas myth going for a very, very long time, for my benefit; I think they thought it was really hilarious. Every year, from when I was born until I was eleven, Cliffy would dress up as Father Christmas in his red suit and sack in one of the spare bedrooms and, when we were in bed, he would go outside and knock on the window. Everyone would always urge him to knock and walk off, in case I spotted it was him, but he would always linger a bit too long because he'd had a few glasses of sherry. I guess I really wanted to believe, and I was determined that it wasn't Cliffy. It wasn't until I was about twelve that I finally clocked that the big man in the red suit with a sack over his shoulder wasn't actually real.

Mum always had the whole family over on Christmas Day, our grandparents, aunts, uncles and cousins, and she would cook the most wonderful meal, with about a million courses. Ba Ba, who only ever drank champagne, was a big one for food-fighting and when all the adults had drunk too much, around the time of the main course, led by Ba Ba, everyone would start lobbing Brussels sprouts across the table at each other! After the Brussels sprouts had run out, we would move on to brie from the cheeseboard and whatever else was going spare. Food would be splattered all over the tablecloth, the walls and over each other. Months later, we would still find errant and mouldy Brussels sprouts hidden under furniture.

Being the youngest, I was always really spoilt when it came to my presents. On Christmas morning, it was like Ba Ba and Cliffy had emptied Hamleys out onto our sitting-room floor. It was a bit obscene, and my dad's mum, my Nana, used to hate it because it was so over-the-top. When I was about three, Ba Ba bought me a pink bicycle with stabilisers and left it in the garage because it was too big to bring inside the house. Mum and Dad actually forgot about it until the end of the day because I had so many presents. It was wrapped

Being the youngest, I was always really spoilt when it came to my presents

really badly, because it was so big, but it was amazing. My brother pushed me down a hill on it without stabilisers – so I learned to ride a bike pretty fast! Barbie featured very heavily on the present front for a number of years because I loved them so much, and one new Barbie meant I could make a whole new family with her. One year I was given a Barbie car where you could pull a barbecue and picnic table out of the boot and it had a special sunroof. It was my favourite car in the world.

During my childhood, I saw a lot of Ba Ba and Cliffy. They'd moved from Dorset, where Mum had spent the latter end of her childhood and her teenage years, and had a lovely, grand house in Richmond. From when I was born, we would go and stay overnight with them almost weekly and we would have wonderful dinners out together. They were very protective of Mum, Ollie, AL and I. I think they realised that Mum and Dad's marriage was starting to flounder and, of course, they were on Mum's side. Ba Ba was so generous and would often take us shopping for new clothes, even if we didn't want to go – she would drag us along and insist on buying things for us. She loved spoiling us and we all had her wrapped round our little fingers. If Mum and Dad said no to something, we would always ask Ba Ba and she would always say yes. We were really cosseted by her. Famously, my brother ran out of money during his first year at university because he had been going out too much and spending all his money on booze, and when Mum and Dad refused to give him any more money for socialising, he rang Ba Ba and she sent him some. He then proceeded to blow it all on a single night out and, for obvious reasons, she wasn't best pleased.

Throughout all of this time, even though life was blissful, Mum and Dad's relationship was becoming more difficult.

Throughout all of this time, even though life was blissful, Mum and Dad's relationship was becoming more difficult

Clearly neither Dad nor Mum were happy in the relationship but I was only a child and at the time I couldn't understand what was going on and why the marriage wasn't a happy one. Some days I used to see Mum crying on her own in the sitting room when she thought no one could see.

44

I remember on another occasion, I was upstairs in my bedroom playing with my Barbies and I heard a wailing sound downstairs. I thought to myself, 'What is that noise?' It didn't sound like normal crying; it was far more raw and painful. I ran down the stairs and saw Mum was in the sitting room, with her back to me. As she turned round, I saw her eyes were red raw and swollen from crying so much and there were loads of tissues scattered around her. I felt so shocked and upset, but didn't know what to say and just hugged her. I remember her holding me so tightly for a long time, before saying, 'Come along, darling, let's have a cup of tea,' and she pulled herself together and stopped crying. We never talked about what was wrong, but I knew it was something to do with her and Dad.

My parents' unhappy marriage was masked when we were all at home together, surrounded by friends. However, things changed when my siblings left home and I really started to see how bad things had got between them. When we sat together for dinner, the atmosphere always felt strained and the conversation was often stilted.

AL went to London and the following year Ollie went backpacking in his gap year to Australia and Kenya. He would send long emails home saying what he was doing, along with loads of photos, and he was quite wild. He married a Maasai warrior in a special ceremony while he was in Africa, although apparently everyone does – or so he said – and I recall one story where he got with this girl who was obsessed with him. She wanted to get a tattoo and asked Ollie to sketch it for her because she was so into him. He drew this design for her and told her that it meant 'love' in another language. It didn't; it was just a squiggle. He sent us this picture of her with this enormous tattoo across the bottom of her leg. She was clearly a bit crazy! He also managed to almost drown while surfing in Australia, when he became caught in a riptide, but his friend Rob and another guy surfed out and saved him.

Ollie was quite arty and, when he came back, he made this huge papier-mâché wave across his bedroom wall and painted it. As a family, we were nicknamed 'the Fellies' by our friends and Ollie wrote 'Fellie's love shack' across the top of the wave. At that time, he was really grumpy and I used to catch him smoking out of the window and he would yell at me to get out, and I would threaten to tell Mum and Dad. I guess he found it difficult being back after the freedom of travelling on his own. He did have his cheerier moods and he would occasionally take me out to the cinema in his car, which he nicknamed 'Punani', which I loved. In my eyes, even if he was moody, he could do no wrong.

Ollie left the following September to go to the University of West England in Bristol. We all helped him pack his things and loaded up the Range Rover and went with him. We helped him move into his new hall of residence, and his room felt so stark and bare. Mum busied herself trying to make it as homely as possible. I was only nine years old, so I didn't really know what university was, but I knew that life at home wouldn't be the same without him. After he was bedded in in his new halls, we went out for lunch together and then said goodbye to him. Going home that night was so strange because it felt so quiet in the car, and when we ate dinner I immediately missed him pinching me or nicking the food off my plate. I felt this horrible, sad feeling in the pit of my stomach. I always hoped he'd call but he never used to telephone home much, despite the fact that Ba Ba had given him a mobile phone with which he ran up extortionate bills. I used to so look forward to him coming home on the odd weekend, counting down the days until he would turn up outside.

After a year, Ollie decided that he wanted to start working on a career rather than continue at university, so he got a job in London, working for various different companies. I would often go with Mum when she went to visit him. He moved straight to Chelsea and shared a house next to the Bluebird restaurant with some friends, who all seemed to be called Ollie. On one occasion, when we were visiting, he was popping out for a sunbed, and all the other Ollies filtered out of the room. Our Ollie was last and, just as he was leaving, he turned and asked if I wanted to go with them. I thought all my birthdays had come at once – I longed to be uber-cool like him.

On another occasion, Mum and I tried to suss out Fulham. We knew Ollie loved it, but neither of us had any idea where anything was because Mum only really knew north-west London. We walked to the Tesco on the Fulham Road and hailed a black cab and we went down the King's Road. After exploring for a couple of hours, we ended up at the Bluebird, where I bought Mum lunch. Everywhere we looked there were glamorous people having fun and it felt really special. I loved it then like I do now.

Back at home, I carried on spending all my free time with my pony and the other animals, trying to ignore the fact that

Mum and Dad were arguing more than ever. A year or two after Ollie moved to London, Dad's company was sold and the board of directors were gradually replaced with a new board, so Dad left to look for new challenges. Mum had told me that there were going to be some changes around the place because Dad had bought a couple of other properties and was looking to launch a coaching inn. She said that we would probably have to move house, and I was really sad about that. Then, a few days later, Dad said he was expecting a call about an even better job than the one he'd had before and we all got really excited, thinking we wouldn't have to move from Endlewick House. I remember AL and Ollie came home for the weekend and Mum took us to the local pub for a drink so Dad could take the call in private at home without being disturbed. I was in a very bad mood, really stroppy, which was pretty standard at that time. It was quite tense being at the pub, but when we got home, Dad had a huge smile on his face. He told us he'd got the job!

However, just a couple of days later, we found out that the job offer had fallen through for some reason and we were back to square one. When Mum broke the news, she told me that while we were going to have to move, we would still have each other. She said we would find somewhere else to live that wouldn't be as big, but that we could keep all the animals and she would try her best to make it a good new home for us. But I knew that things would never be the same again.

But I knew that things would never be the same again

My favourite places

Other than Chelsea and Fulham, there are a few other places that I love. I normally stay with friends or family when I go away, but here are some suggestions of where to plan a holiday or break away:

 Méribel, France: This is a wonderful place to go skiing and we've had some brilliant holidays there in the past few years. The après-ski here is the best. I love the club La Folie Douce (www.lafoliedouce.com), on the side of the mountain, and we have spent many afternoons there – it's Jägerbombs galore and everyone pouring vodka from the highest of heights into each other's mouths. The difficult thing is getting back down the mountain if you miss the last bubble lift at around 6 p.m. It's always quite entertaining skiing down with the family after an afternoon there drinking trying not to fall or crash into each other. For after-hours clubbing, there is the legendary Dick's Tea Bar, Le Loft and Le Poste de Secours in Méribel town centre.

 Rock, Cornwall: I really loved our holidays in Rock when I was a kid. It's changed quite a lot now and isn't really the same as it used to be. Now the

Mariners is a wine bar. I like going to a bar called the Oystercatcher in Polzeath (www.oystercatcherpolzeath.co.uk); it has a young atmosphere and there is often a live band playing. It feels a bit like going back to the old days because there are loads of good-looking boys hanging out there.

 New York: I went to New York recently for a work opportunity and stayed at the Grand Hyatt off Fifth Avenue (www.grandnewyork.hyatt.com), which was amazing – and absolutely massive! New York is great for a Christmas trip because the Americans overdo everything and it looks so magical with lights strung up everywhere. It goes without saying that the shopping is incredible. My sister AL is now living near Central Park and I'm looking forward to many trips going to visit her and her dog, Ruby, who flew across the pond with her in her own special doggy cage!

 Ibiza: Ibiza is glorious. Last year I went to No.1 Boot Camp there in the north of the island (www.no1bootcamp.com). Every night we would go to one of the quieter, more peaceful beaches and drink from coconuts and watch the sun dip down behind the mountains in the distance.

There was music playing, hippies were dancing around and everyone was happy. If you're going with friends, there are obviously all the big clubs, like Pacha, Space and Amnesia, further south, but I am happy to stick to the north of the island. I'd love to do a *Made in Chelsea* special there.

 East Sussex: This is my home, and I adore this part of the world. There are loads of pretty and tranquil villages to visit and stunning scenery across the South Downs. I used to work at a beautiful restaurant called the Wingrove (www.wingrovehousealfriston.com), which also has some rooms, and there are lots of great walks nearby.

South Africa: At the end of last year I went there to film some episodes of *Made in Chelsea* and we got to go on safari and see some of the 'Big Five'. It was an incredible experience to see what life is like in the bush and one of my personal highlights was cuddling gorgeous lion cubs. We stayed in this glorious country lodge, a few hours from Johannesburg, where the scenery was breathtaking.

4

A LONG AND
UNHAPPY ROAD

'We've decided to buy a pub. It will be a new start for all of us,' Mum said to me one day after school, when I was about twelve years old.

With Dad out of work, Mum knew they had to find a way to earn some money and she thought that owning a pub would be the solution to their financial worries because they could both work behind the bar to help make ends meet. Eventually, after looking through lots of estate agents' brochures, they found an old pub called the Best Beech, which was in a village called Wadhurst in East Sussex. The property had some rooms above the bar, so also served as a bed and breakfast, and there was a cottage next door for the landlords to live in.

However, rather than staying on the grounds, Mum wanted to try to recreate a family home, so they also bought a little house eight miles from the inn, called Tott Cottage. Our animals came with us and my pony at that time, who was called

Ash, went to live in a nearby livery yard, so I could keep riding him after school if I had time and during the weekends and holidays. I know my parents didn't have much money, but Mum was determined for me to keep Ash, which, looking back, I am so grateful for.

It was around this time that I started occasionally staying overnight at the school I was at, St Andrew's. They had boarders there, so it never seemed like a big deal. I don't think Mum and Dad wanted me to be around when we finally shut the door to Endlewick House forever and it suited them because I was so well looked after at school.

The first time I went to Tott Cottage, which was in a village called Burwash, near Tunbridge Wells, Ba Ba picked me up from school and drove me there in her car. She kept muttering, 'It'll all be all right darlin',' which is what she always used to say to me. I had that horrible sick feeling at the back of my throat and my stomach was doing somersaults. The new house felt cold, empty and unloved. Don't get me wrong, it was perfectly fine and easily big enough for the three of us and all the animals, but it didn't feel like home in the way Endlewick House had.

I had that horrible sick feeling at the back of my throat and my stomach was doing somersaults

Initially I was quite excited about Mum and Dad owning a pub, as they had sold the idea to me quite well. They told me my friends could come and stay and that it would be really fun, and I went along with it. I remember the first time I went to the pub it really smelt of beer and cigarettes and, soon after, reality hit that it wasn't the most glorious thing in the world. Mum and Dad hadn't realised how hard it would be to run a pub and everything that it would entail. Mum was working in any job she could to keep us afloat. She had two jobs in Brighton – one was working for one of her cousins and the other was helping out at a florist – and then she and Dad would take it in turns to man the bar in the evenings until late.

I also had to change schools, as it wasn't possible to commute backwards and forwards from St Andrew's. I enrolled in an all-girls' day and boarding school called Bedgebury, which was nearby. At first, it felt a bit weird not having any boys around because I had always been to mixed schools before then. It was a bit daunting and scary to be the new girl, but I soon made friends and settled in. It was a really supportive environment and the girls were really friendly and modest. No one worried about make-up, fashion, boys or anything like that.

No one worried about make-up, fashion, boys or anything like that

However, my home life was difficult. With the strain of Dad changing his career, Mum and Dad's relationship had broken down completely and they were barely speaking. Mum was under a lot of pressure holding down her various jobs. Initially the plan was that they would take it in turns to look after me, with me staying at home with Dad on the evenings when Mum was working, but Dad and I argued constantly. I can see now that he was trying to make it fun by planning ideas like recreating *Ready Steady Cook* in our kitchen at Tott Cottage, but he would just tell me what to do and wouldn't listen to me or ask me what I wanted to do. I hated it. It wasn't helped by the fact that I knew he and Mum weren't speaking. I felt so protective of Mum and I didn't want to be away from her.

In the end, I would go to the pub with Mum on the nights that she was working. After going to see my pony Ash after school, we would head to the pub and in the car we used to listen to this album full of feel-good songs and we would sing along as loudly as we could, until our throats were sore, to try to make ourselves *I felt so protective of Mum and I didn't want to be away from her* feel better about the situation. As we pulled up outside the Best Beech and got out of the car, Mum would give me a big cuddle and a kiss before we went inside, and I would go up the back stairs to one of the bedrooms. I wasn't allowed in the pub itself because I was too young. The upstairs rooms were plain and sparsely furnished. I always went to the same one – number four – where there was a double bed, bedside tables, a dressing table and a small TV. I would start on my homework, and often just doodled in my notepad to pass the time. I remember eating a lot of chicken and thyme Walkers Sensation crisps. Even now, the smell of those crisps takes me straight back to that pub.

Sometimes, when I was really bored, I would go downstairs and try to talk to the washer-upper, James, who was a few years older and a son of one of the local families. The key was getting down the stairs to the kitchen without being found out. If Dad saw me, he would get really angry. Sometimes I tried reading books, but I was never particularly into reading, so I would twiddle my thumbs until Mum's shift finished at gone 11 p.m., when we would drive home and I would finally go to bed, pretty exhausted. The head chef used to live in the cottage attached to the pub and he had a four-year-old daughter whom I would babysit from time to time. The girl was a bit of a nightmare and quite bratty, but being in a homely environment was much better. We would watch TV and have dinner together and it wasn't so bad when I was there because I felt responsible and like I had some sort of purpose.

My feelings all came to a head one weekend when my sister came home to see us. She was having an amazing time in London and was full of stories of what she was doing, the people she was meeting and all the boys she was being introduced to. By then, Ollie and AL visited rarely because they didn't want to be around Mum and Dad and the terrible mood at home. I was depressed and angry and so envious of their freedom. We had a massive argument before we left the house to go to the pub. It was because of something completely ridiculous, the fact that I was wearing too much make-up. I was a fan of this hideous blue, sparkly eye shadow at the time and thought I might see James and that it would look good. If I could get downstairs for long enough, we would flirt and, quite frankly, that was about as exciting as it got because there wasn't much else do.

When we arrived, I was sent upstairs to the bedroom that I used to hang out in, while everyone else was at the bar. I felt

I was depressed and angry and so envious of their freedom

so left out. The room was directly above the bar and, because it was such an old pub, you could hear everything through the rickety floorboards. I was so angry about the situation and just lost it. I was screaming and stamping and I just couldn't stop crying. I felt horrible. Perhaps my situation doesn't sound so terrible to a lot of people, but I felt so lost and frustrated with everything; it felt like my whole life was falling apart. AL came up and hugged me, but I hated the fact that she was going back to London and could escape what was now a fairly miserable existence. She stroked my back while I cried and, not long afterwards, Mum came up. She was sobbing as she hugged me. She said, 'This is going to be the beginning of a long road of unhappiness.' I don't think either of us could see any way that things could get better for us.

It was clear that Mum and Dad's relationship was worse than ever. We had one Christmas at Tott Cottage and although Ollie and AL came home to celebrate with us like they did every year, it wasn't like our normal traditional Christmases, like the ones at Endlewick House. Mum did her best to decorate Tott Cottage like the old house, with a tree and cards displayed everywhere, but the cottage wasn't big enough for all our family to sit round the table for lunch and although people popped in and out throughout the day, it just wasn't the same. The atmosphere was awful and so strained. Mum and Dad barely said one word to each other. I think they were really starting to hate each other.

By then, Ba Ba was living in a huge flat on the Brighton seafront. Cliffy had passed away at the grand old age of ninety-four, after declaring at ninety-two that he was bored of their life in Richmond, so they had moved to a flat on the Brighton seafront for his final days and he died just before our first Christmas at Tott Cottage. We still saw a lot of Ba Ba and we were incredibly close. She would come to the pub, looking very glamorous, and sit and have a drink at the bar, watching the world go past and chatting to some of the locals. When Cliffy died, it was very sad, and while Ba Ba tried to keep her spirits up and not show how heartbroken she was, she never really managed to get back to her old self. Her eyes always looked sad, even though she tried to be cheery.

Ba Ba herself was old and I knew her health wasn't great. Fifteen months after Cliffy died, she went into hospital to have a routine operation, but she had to stay there because there had been some sort of complication during the procedure. Mum had told my school what was happening and asked if I could board for a while, so she could go and be with her, and they were happy for me to stay overnight.

One evening, after we had returned from a school trip to the beach, I was sitting outside with some of my friends, watching the sun set. The sky was blue and yellow and really stunning, like a postcard. As we sat there, chatting and gossiping, this huge, glinting stream of white and silver light arced across the sky on the horizon and I thought to myself, 'Someone must've died.' I was really quiet and thoughtful for a while, which was quite rare for me because I was normally so chatty. I didn't for a second think that Ba Ba could've passed away. To me, she was far too strong and alive to ever not be around. I just couldn't imagine life without her being there, cuddling me and telling me everything would be OK. I thought she would live forever.

The next day was a Saturday and I was sitting on the school steps, clutching my bag, waiting to be picked up. As I saw our car roll up the long driveway, I noticed that AL and Ollie were with Mum, which I thought was a bit strange. Ollie got out of the passenger seat and, as soon as he did, I could tell by the look on his face that something was horribly wrong. He just hugged me and simply said, 'Ba Ba has died.' I couldn't believe it and dissolved into tears. I sobbed into his shoulder and all four of us cried together as we made the journey back to her flat in Brighton. By then, Ollie was becoming the man of the house and I was glad that it was him who had told me because I had such respect for him, but it felt like such a hole in my life.

Mum and her Uncle Brian – Ba Ba's brother – organised the funeral. It was held in Brighton and there was a huge turnout, including some of my sister's ex-boyfriends, who had got to know Ba Ba over the years, neighbours, family friends and colleagues. We were standing at the front of the church and I was flanked by AL and Ollie, and Mum was standing next to Ollie. It was horrific because we were all so upset. My brother was digging his nails into his hands, almost drawing blood, because he didn't want to cry, which made me feel even worse. My mum was in bits, holding a gold crucifix in her hand and trying to stop the tears from flowing. Somehow we got through the funeral, but it was dreadfully hard. Afterwards we went back to the flat, where there was an amazing spread of food, but no one felt like eating anything. We played some upbeat music, but we all felt horrible.

A while afterwards, when Mum's aunt came to visit, we

took Ba Ba's and Cliffy's ashes to the South Downs. There was a point in the landscape where they wanted to have their ashes thrown off the hills. Loads of family and friends drove in a convoy down there with us. We always took the mick in my family and anyone was fair game. As my brother mixed the bags of ashes together and they flew off in the wind, he made some stupid jokes like 'There goes Ba Ba's nose and here's one of Cliffy's fingers.' Everyone was laughing at him. It was like he always knew what to say at difficult moments.

It was at that time that Mum decided to leave Dad for good and go and live in Ba Ba's flat in Brighton, which had been left to her. By then, things had got so bad between my parents, there was no going back and when Mum told Dad she was leaving, he was angry and they had another heated argument. A few days later, I remember him coming to the Brighton flat to say he was sorry about Ba Ba and he was like a changed person and was being funny, kind and interested. For some time, he would come to the flat every night and AL would put me to bed and sit by Mum's side, so Dad couldn't say anything to her. I know AL felt hugely protective of Mum too and, because she was older, probably understood more than I did at the time about what was going on. One night Mum agreed to go for a drink to talk to him about it at a nearby hotel, but she had to sit and wait for him and was really cross. Eventually a group of people she knew saw she was on her own and invited her to join them for some drinks. When Dad did turn up at 10.30 p.m. he was combative and that was it, the relationship was over. It was the final nail in the coffin.

I know there are two sides to every story, but because of

my closeness to her, I was on Mum's side during the split. I didn't have anything to do with Dad for a year after that incident.

My brother tried so hard for me to keep in touch with Dad because, out of all of us, they spoke the most and have always been close. Ollie once sent me a text message he had clearly meant to send to Dad, saying, 'I've tried speaking to her. Don't worry, I will keep on trying and you will have her back again.' Ollie knew that I listened to everything he said and respected him, but on this occasion, I wasn't going to do what he wanted. As far as I was concerned, I was old enough to make my own decisions.

Christmas became a big point of contention with Dad because AL, Ollie and I would always spend the day with Mum and he wanted to see us. One year I wanted a new pair of boots and they were really expensive. Dad came round to the flat in Brighton after being at a dinner party with close family friends of both his and Mum's. He came up in the lift, but Mum wouldn't allow him in the flat. As I answered the door, I could see that he had been in tears and in his arms there was this big present, which I instantly knew was the boots that I wanted.

Christmas became a big point of contention with Dad

'I'm not staying, I'm not staying,' he said, as he passed it over, sobbing. I crumpled into tears.

'I don't know what to do,' I said.

He turned round and left, going back to his dinner party. When I eventually opened the present on Christmas morning, it was exactly the boots that I wanted. I felt so torn and guilty that he would be on his own. He was my Dad and I still loved him.

The other big problem at the time was that we were quite a long way from my school, Bedgebury, so we decided that I should become a weekly boarder. Mum and I had become so close during our time in Brighton. Most days, after my parent's divorce, it felt like it was her and me against the world. When we were in Ba Ba's flat, we used to share her big double bed together and say to each other, 'It's you and me again. You and me against the world.' We used to speak to each other in silly accents, which would make us laugh, and even now we still do it, along with my stepsisters, who came into my life after this time. We found that we could vocalise things that we probably didn't feel we could say ordinarily.

Mum would drive me to Bedgebury every Sunday night and I would stay there until the following Friday, when she would pick me up again. I was properly homesick. I had stayed overnight at school before, when I was at St Andrew's, but with my parents' split and Ba Ba's death, I just felt lost.

I would be happy in lessons during the day – or as happy as I could be at school – but in the evenings, I would just lose it because I wanted to be with Mum and missed her dreadfully. I worried about her, after everything that had happened with Dad.

I couldn't sleep in the dark and would wake up, not remembering where I was and feeling so disorientated, thinking that I had gone blind. Mum bought me these glow-in-the-dark stars that I stuck on the ceiling and a small nightlight that I put by my bed. The girls that I shared with were really sweet and didn't mind the lamp being on. The boarding staff were also really good with me and I used to speak to the housemistress every night for hours before I went to bed because I was so upset. When I was allowed to use my mobile phone at night, I would hear my mum's voice and be unable to speak because I missed her so much and was crying so hard. She would try everything to stop me from being so upset and, for a while, even took the hard-line approach, saying, 'You've got to stop it and pull yourself together, Binky. You're not helping anyone by being like this,' but that would make me even worse, so she had to go back to being sympathetic. I shouldn't really have spoken to her at all, as each time I did, I went back to square one. Looking back, I now realise how awful it must've been for her to hear me like that every day.

I called her at every opportunity and would quickly run out of credit on my mobile phone and panic that I wouldn't be able to speak to her for a few days. I would beg the other girls for their phones and at first they were happy to lend *I felt like a real loner* them to me, but after a few weeks they got fed up that I was using up all their credit, crying down the phone. I was totally miserable and I think all the girls I shared with got bored of my tears. I felt like a real loner.

To help me cope, I made this huge piece of paper with 'Monday, Tuesday, Wednesday, Thursday, Friday' written across the top, and I would tick off the days with a huge black marker pen until I could be back with Mum again.

Mum seemed to be the one constant in my life and not being with her made me feel so lonely and insecure. I would always tell her, 'Love you,' and she would reply, 'Love you more.'

I know Mum felt awful about the situation too and did everything she could to make me feel happier when I was away during the week. She bought me a hamster called Bubbles. There was a pet shed at Bedgebury and I already had my rabbit, Thumper, there, who had loads of babies, which I went on to sell to some of the other girls. I couldn't transport a big case every weekend, so Mum made Bubbles her very own bespoke one, with a huge handle. Bubbles was a bit of an escape artist, so Mum got a plastic sheet and sewed it round the bag, with a flap for me to open. When she finished making it, she got a marker pen and wrote 'Gucci' and 'Prada' on it – so it looked like Bubbles had her own designer travelling bag. This poor hamster was virtually suffocating inside this plastic travelling bag. No wonder I wasn't popular! I think Bubbles wasn't a huge fan of the bag either and, once, she even managed to escape to the bottom of the loo in the Brighton flat. AL found her, at first thinking it was a furry poo, and then realising it was my pet she scooped Bubbles out and revived her. Despite the fact that things were hard, we always managed to laugh.

The flat was full of our animals, although by then it was just Tatiana, my Westie; Harvey Nichols, the Labrador; and Spagic, the cat. I kept my pony at a nearby livery yard and was so happy that I could still have him. Dad was never particularly bothered about the animals, but they were like

Mum's surrogate children, so one day, after we had left, he just dropped them off to live with us. The flat was located in Crescent Place, which is practically on the seafront. It was beautiful and homely and had an enormous balcony, where we laid some grass, so it felt like a bit of a garden for the animals. We would take the dogs for long walks along the beach, but I know it wasn't ideal for them. Mum or I – mostly Mum – would have to walk them multiple times a day because we didn't have a proper garden. By then, Spagic the cat was really old and couldn't walk very well. We gave him to one of my friends to look after, but we missed him so much we asked for him back. He used to chill on the balcony in the sun and lick his paws.

I've always been really ditsy and forgetful and I remember one day I popped out to the local shops to buy something and took Tatiana with me. I couldn't take her inside the shop, so I tied her to a lamppost outside with her lead and off I went inside on my errand. It was only a couple of hours later, when I was back at home lying on the sofa watching some TV and the phone rang, that I realised I had forgotten Tatiana. A tramp had found her outside the shop and had taken her with him. I was mortified and promptly burst into tears. My poor dog! AL was staying with us at the time and I was so terrified of the angry tramp that I made her go and pick Tatiana up from him. Apparently he gave her such an earful – and it wasn't even her fault.

Despite all the upheaval, when Mum and I were living at Ba Ba's flat, it was quite a happy time for us. With the strain of Dad being around and their difficult relationship no longer an everyday issue, it felt like a weight had been lifted off everyone's shoulders. We were surrounded by all of Ba Ba's things, so it felt like home and like she was still there. My friend Letty would come and stay and, before we scattered Ba Ba's and Cliffy's ashes across the Downs, we would put the urns on the table and we would all sit and have dinner, then watch TV together.

Letty was probably thinking, 'This is pretty weird,' but being such a good friend, she never mentioned it.

I would also go and stay with her family when I was living in London, which was a real escape for me. They were quite a different family to ours; her parents were often not around during the day. We weren't allowed to watch much TV, so spent most of our time outside in the countryside, going on long bike rides and playing on the trampoline in the garden. Sometimes we would choreograph dances, dress up in stupid clothes and make silly videos of ourselves.

Back in Kent, the boarding situation wasn't getting any better. I was constantly on the phone in tears and would be inconsolable for hours before I was due back at the boarding house every Sunday night. It was like that Sunday night feeling most people get before a working week, but a hundred times worse. While the other girls were kind and sweet, I never really made friendships like the one I had with Letty. In the end, Mum decided that I should go to a school nearer to the flat and I was delighted about it. I hoped that it would be the start of a completely new chapter for me. Little did I know then that it was going to be a very memorable time, but for all the wrong reasons.

Coping with your parents' divorce

Whatever the situation or reasons for divorce, it's a very hard thing to go through if you're a child, teenager or even an adult. If, like me, your parents decide to part ways when you're a teenager, it's a time of great change anyway. Things can be even more difficult if you are particularly close to one parent.

Remember it's not your fault

A divorce is never the fault of the children. Parents are adults and they can emotionally manipulate you and may tell you things that really upset you. The more time goes by, the more you will understand. And you may never understand, but that's OK too.

Take care of yourself

Try to focus on your hobbies or whatever it is that you enjoy away from your home life. I felt riding and being outdoors was the best escape for me, but whether you love sports, music or reading, these things can really help take your mind off the split.

Talk about it with others

You will have a lot of feelings regarding your parents' split, so it may be helpful to talk to a good friend or trusted adult about the situation if you need to. Shock, anger, guilt, relief because your parents had been fighting a lot and sadness are all normal emotions.

Don't worry about the future
Try not to worry about what hasn't happened yet. If there is something, like an occasion, that is coming up that you are particularly concerned about, talk to one of your parents and you can come up with a solution together. Remember that what will be, will be.

Know that your parents may act differently
It's to be expected that your parents will also be suffering and so will act differently for a while. This has nothing to do with you; it is just their way of coping. Sometimes one parent may want to split while the other doesn't. They didn't get married expecting things not to work out, so this is their way of grieving for the relationship they have lost.

Everyone's experience is different
Divorce affects everyone differently, depending on his or her personality and family life. I loved my life before my parents' split, but now I can see clearly that it was for the best. No matter what you feel, it's OK. Just remember that no two experiences are alike, so try not to compare your experience to that with a friend's.

5

FACING THE BULLIES

After Mum agreed that I could leave Bedgebury so I could live at home, I started as a day girl at St Mary's Hall, a school just a few streets away from Ba Ba's flat in Brighton. When we first looked around the school, I didn't care what it was like or if the teachers and girls seemed nice; I just wanted to be back at the flat with Mum. School and learning always seemed an uphill struggle and made me anxious, regardless of where I was. I had a couple of assessments carried out by education and learning specialists, who all agreed that my learning difficulties made school a pretty gruelling time for me.

On my first day at St Mary's, after I was shown into my new classroom, I quickly realised that the girls were completely different from the ones I had been with at Bedgebury and St Andrew's. They wore loads of make-up and tiny skirts and were all having sex at thirteen. They were really quite hard. It was unlike anything I had known before, having grown up with country kids and not caring about what I wore.

I remember looking at my shoes and thinking, 'I'm wearing Kickers and everyone else is wearing heels,' and looking around to see that every girl had at least a brush of mascara on, whereas I was completely make-up free. I also had hideous braces, as my front teeth stuck out because I had sucked my thumb for a long time. I was a complete geek in comparison to the other girls.

I was a complete geek in comparison to the other girls

As soon as I arrived, they made it clear that I was an outsider. During the first week, when it came to registration time, there were groups of girls sitting together and a single chair on its own, where I soon realised I was meant to sit. No one talked to me or made an effort to include me in their conversations. I immediately felt very uncomfortable and started to tally up in my head how long I would have to be there.

Most of the popular girls would all hang out together in one big group. There were a few other smaller groups of girls, but they also weren't like me, for different reasons. The popular group was the one I longed to be a part of. It was just like the film *Mean Girls*, and I soon became their target. The bullying didn't happen straightaway, but soon after I arrived, I started to realise that the way I was being treated by them wasn't a case of petty teenage rows. I longed to fit in, and tried to, but the girls didn't want to know.

In the first few weeks I would go on MSN Messenger on my computer after school and we would have these big group conversations and they would often say bitchy things about me. If I spelt something wrong, which happened a lot, they would always take the piss out of me and call me thick. The way the messaging system was set up meant that there could be multiple conversations going on at the same time and it was clear that some of girls were having their own private conversations about me on the side, which I couldn't see.

The girls used to throw things at me across the classroom, say nasty things about me behind my back and, in the way only young girls can, they would pretend to be my friend and suddenly hate me again five minutes later. They would agree to meet me somewhere and, when I arrived, I would see them all huddled together, laughing, before they ran away. At lunchtimes, they would throw my tray on the floor, so my food went everywhere, and I would be left on my hands and knees, trying to pick everything up. Every morning I'd go and sit in my chair and keep my head down to avoid the smirks. After registration, we would go to chapel for assembly and, by that point, I just couldn't keep the tears in and would sob as quietly as I could during the hymns. I just couldn't stop myself.

At one time, I seemed to get in with the cool crew and some of the girls started talking to me and including me in what they did, but the leader, who was called Jessica, seemed to get jealous of my growing popularity and turned them all against me by making things up about me and saying that if they talked to me, she would blank them. It made my life really difficult. From time to time, after that, I would try to befriend one of the group individually. There was a girl called Anna, whom everyone adored because she was so sweet and kind. She didn't have a bad bone in her body. She used to be so lovely to me when it was just the two of us, but as soon as the girls realised what was going on, they would shout at her, 'C'mon, Anna, why are you with her?'

'I'm sorry, I have to go with them,' she would say, looking guilty and worried.

'It's fine. I don't want you getting into trouble with them too,' I would reply, feeling more upset than before. It was a total pack mentality and I knew what Anna was up against. It was much better to be part of it than be on the outside. I longed to be accepted by them.

I was still struggling with my learning difficulty and the girls also used to bully me for being stupid in lessons. I was always bottom of the class, in all the bottom sets, and never understood much at all about what we were being taught. I was terrified of putting my hand up to ask a question if I didn't understand something because I knew they would scream at me: 'Why are you holding us back?'; 'Oh for God's sake, you're so stupid, why are you so thick?'; or 'Why don't you get it?' Eventually, I started to have private one-to-one lessons at lunch in the subjects I was struggling with and, far from finding it a chore, I was thrilled about it because lunchtime was one of the worst periods of the day. I had no friends to hang out with and would go to the loo for ages, to try to avoid the horrible girls. In these classes, I went over the basics, such as simple sums in maths,

I was still struggling with my learning difficulty and the girls also used to bully me

which was my worst subject. The girls used to tease me about my private lessons and would wait outside the block and scream abuse at me as I left, like: 'What have you been learning today? Two plus two?'

I remember one occasion, when I came out of one of my extra lessons, and three or four girls appeared from nowhere and started taunting me, yelling, 'Thicko, you're so stupid, you shouldn't even be at this school, you're so dumb.' I didn't know what to do or say and just walked as quickly as I could in the opposite direction, trying to look as if I didn't care what they were saying about me.

There was a girl called Sophie who was one of the big personalities in the group. One day after school, I was on MSN Messenger and she logged in and started a conversation, saying, 'I don't want to do this to you any more. You're not a bad person. Let's put everything that has happened to one side. Tomorrow, at school, we'll say sorry to you and all have a big hug and be friends again!' I felt really excited for the first time in ages about going to school. I ran downstairs to the kitchen, where Mum was cooking, and relayed what Sophie had said to me on MSN. I was so delighted and relieved about it.

'They have made peace with me, Mum,' I told her, all smiles. 'Everything is going to change at school. They want to be friends with me.'

I couldn't believe it had finally happened and they would accept me as one of the gang, but Mum didn't look particularly happy. In fact, she looked really concerned.

'Do you know what today is, darling?' she replied.

'No, what?'

'It's April the first – April Fool's Day.'

She grabbed me and hugged me, and I burst into tears and cried for a long time. She told me to ignore them and I tried, but it was so hard. The next day nothing had changed, of course, and it went back to exactly how it had been with the taunting, shouting and stupid pranks they played on me. For a long time, it felt like things like that happened every day; one incident seemed to roll into another and then into another. That doesn't stand out as being particularly cruel; there were many incidents like that one.

I felt lower than ever, but despite wanting to be part of the group, I knew I wasn't like them and I was proud of that fact. The thing that kept me going was believing in myself and knowing that, when school was over, I would make something of my life. Hopefully, I would live in London, have lots of friends and, most of all, I'd be a decent person. I wanted to be like my big brother – I wanted to be a success, be *somebody*. He was living the high life in Fulham, with all his gorgeous friends. He had a City job and a flash car that he drove everywhere. He would come home occasionally and get drunk and make Mum and me laugh, and he would tell me that I could come and live with him when I was old enough and that he would take me out with all his friends and look after me. He made me feel so loved. He gave me hope and he did exactly what he'd promised when I did eventually move to London after school. At that time, he was always there for me, like a knight in shining armour.

I wanted to be a success, be somebody

Every day at school, I would count down the hours until I could go home. I would run home through the Brighton streets and be so happy to get through the front door of the flat. I told Mum everything about what was happening, and every day I would be crying about something someone had said or done to me. Mum had some experience of bullying because AL was also bullied when she was at school, when girls were horrible to her and would do things like put chewing gum in her hair, but I know now that seeing me so upset was really hard for her.

Eventually, after yet another huge episode with Jessica, Mum went to see the headmistress, whose son was one of the boys who had saved my brother in Australia, so they already knew one another. The headmistress called a meeting with Jessica and her father and we had to sit round a big table and discuss what had happened and why. It was awful. Jessica was crying because her dad was on my side, but of course it didn't make the situation any better, and probably made it worse. In the end, after many heart-to-hearts, Mum took me out of school two months before the summer holidays and St Mary's Hall agreed the plan was for the best. I had been there for less than a year.

After that, Mum asked me if I wanted to talk to a counsellor and I agreed, which I knew she was surprised by. I think she was aware that, with everything that had happened – Ba Ba's death, my parents' split and then the bullying – combined with normal teenage emotions, things might end disastrously. Mum sent me to a counsellor twice a week for a few months, which helped me. I talked about everything that had happened with Mum and Dad and I offloaded about the girls at school and what they had done and said to me. I spoke a lot about how I missed my old life at Endlewick House, when AL and Ollie were still living there. Most of the time, the counsellor just listened to what I said and asked questions, but she sometimes asked me to do exercises to help me process my feelings. One of these was to try to see the situation in pictures. She started by asking me to imagine my life being like a bull in a china shop. She would ask how much of the china was broken, whether there was anything left on the shelf and whether things could be glued back together. I told her everything was broken, but she was helpful. She made me see the good things and, slowly but surely, the picture started to take shape and everything didn't feel so out of control. Talking to her made me appreciate everything a lot more. I knew that I would never take anything for granted ever again. I never do now; I know how lucky I am. I also know I can face challenges head-on because I am confident I will come through the other side.

In the two months I was away from school before the long summer holiday, Mum and I talked about moving back to the country, to try to recreate the life that we used to have back there. We sold the Brighton flat very quickly and Ba Ba had left Mum some money, so we could afford a new house. I knew it wouldn't be like the old one, but we both hoped that we could find something a bit like it in the same area. We spent the evenings and weekends driving back to Sussex from London and trawling through estate agents' brochures, and it gave me hope that things would work out.

We're very spiritual. I believe that somebody is looking after me. We often went to a spiritual church in Brighton when we lived there. I believe in the saying 'What is meant to be will be.' One day I'm going to get it tattooed on my body. Some people don't like this way of thinking and question why bad stuff happens. While I can't explain that, I like to think that if things go belly-up,

We're very spiritual. I believe that somebody is looking after me

there's a reason for that and you'll become a stronger person as a result. There's always something better around the corner. I made myself believe that then, and I still do now. I think that when we die, we don't disappear but go to a different place, and I often feel that Ba Ba is looking out for me. I know she would love *Made in Chelsea* and would be proud of me.

One day Mum and I drove past this house called Lilac Cottage, on the other side of the South Downs to where we had lived before. Mum had always wanted to be on the other side of the Downs and, by a stroke of luck, it had a huge 'For Sale' sign up outside and we immediately booked an appointment to go and see it. It felt like fate. Walking through the front door and looking around, it was like being embraced in a big, warm hug. It was seventeenth century and had loads of character, with wooden beams and fireplaces and a cosy kitchen with an Aga, like a smaller version of Endlewick House. I remember Mum and I praying that we would get it, even though initially Mum thought it would be too expensive. When our offer was accepted by the vendors, we were both over the moon. It felt like our luck was turning and that it really was meant to be.

The final piece of the jigsaw was to find a nearby school for me. We looked around a lot of different ones and many wouldn't even consider having me because of my learning disability. We ended up at St Bede's, the senior school attached to the junior school I had attended as a child. It was a school full of proper country bumpkins, with everyone talking about horses and the latest farm show. Lots of my friends from St Andrew's, like Letty, were pupils there, so we knew it would be a good place for me and I would already have friends there. I remember looking round – it was just beautiful – and having an interview with two teachers, which was really intense. Since I was young, I have always known that I have to impress on the strength of my personality, rather than my brains, so I talked about how much I loved art and the fact that I used to be local to the area and was desperate to be back. Waiting to be accepted was so painful and nerve-wracking and the time seemed to tick past so slowly. Sitting in the flat in Brighton, waiting for the phone to ring, was agonising. I don't think I've ever wanted anything quite so much before. When the phone finally did ring and Mum answered, I knew it was good news when she screamed, 'Yeeeees!' We hugged and cuddled for ages. It was the best feeling in the world. It finally felt like everything was clicking back into place.

I have always known that I have to impress on the strength of my personality

Dealing with hard times and coping with bullying

Talk to someone

I really found that talking to Mum helped when I was being bullied at school, but if you don't want to talk to your parents, talk to a trusted friend or a sympathetic teacher. Seeing a counsellor doesn't mean there is something wrong with you. I found that talking to someone who had no connection to my family life really helped me get through a difficult period of my life. Counselling is often offered in schools. There are also loads of websites and organisations that can help, including www.beatbullying.org.

Try to focus on something else

I love horses and being outside and found that having another focus outside of school and away from the bullies really helped me. So do whatever it is you love doing and try to forget about the bullies for a few hours every day if you can. Don't dwell on the things they say because they are not true.

Try to avoid the bullies

If you can, try to avoid being in situations where you know the bullies will be, like certain places at school. Try your best to avoid them without showing them that you are. When they do say something which makes you feel uncomfortable, try not to react, however hard that is. Bullies gain satisfaction from making others feel hurt or uncomfortable, so giving them a reaction will only encourage them even further. The bully wants attention and if you show them they are emotionally hurting you, they will get more pleasure. Remember that bullies want to show you that they have power, but actually they are cowards and are weak.

Be proud of who you are

Despite what the bullies say, never lose touch with the reasons why you are great. I always held on to the belief that everything would work out well in the long run and would move to London and have a good life and be someone. Remember to believe in who you are.

Listen to happy music

I know it sounds stupid, but I would turn up the stereo really loudly to try to cheer myself up and often it really did help. So turn the music up and sing along.

Don't bottle up your feelings

Having a good cry can make you feel better. Bottling up
your emotions is really unhealthy.

Concentrate on the good things

Try to focus on the parts of your life that you appreciate,
including your friends, family and your good qualities.
Ask the people closest to you what they like about you
and make a list and refer to it whenever you are down.

Keep your sense of humour

Even when things seem really awful, try to laugh. Mum and
I would find humour even in the most ridiculous things, but
it really helped us. Sometimes we would just lie on the floor
and make ridiculous noises to make each other giggle.

Believe it will be OK

Hold on to the fact that it will all be OK in the end. What
seems awful at the time will be a distant memory in
years to come.

6

MY NEW FAMILY AND LONDON LIFE

With our new home, Lilac Cottage, and a new school to attend, life slowly started to feel more normal. I was thirteen by then, so joined the second year at St Bede's, but I quickly slotted back in with my friends from St Andrew's. I moved my pony, who was called Hot Toddy, to Letty's livery yard, which is something we had both dreamt of and talked about for years when we were kids. Hot Toddy was a chestnut gelding and was like a horse version of me because he was really naughty.

Letty and I spent all our spare time hacking out and schooling our ponies together and had loads of fun, laughing all the time. Her pony, Poppy, was also really badly behaved and on many occasions, when we were riding out on the Downs, the horses would just take off and we would be crying with laughter and our arms would feel like jelly, so we were completely unable to stop them.

Letty used to do really amusing stuff, like forget to do up

her girth, so she would mount Poppy and then slide all the way round her tummy and fall off the other side. One of my favourite stories was when we were planning to go for a hack together. Letty was ready and already on Poppy and I was just picking out Toddy's feet, and asked her to hold him while I did his back hooves, so he didn't run off. She agreed and I gave her the reins, but she was busy texting on her phone and as I went to pick up one of his back legs, he bolted off out of the yard and down the road. We really panicked. Letty got off Poppy and put her in her stable, so we could get some food to put into a bucket and shake to coax Toddy back into the yard. However, Letty forgot to bolt the door, so as we ran after Toddy, Poppy – who was totally in love with Toddy – bombed off out of the stable after him too. Letty and I were in full riding gear – chaps, helmets, body protectors and gloves – and really couldn't move very fast and, by that point, we were swearing a lot, knowing that we were going to be in a lot of trouble when our parents found out. Both horses were now galloping down the road towards a junction of a main road and us two idiots were sprinting as fast as we could after them, all sweaty, shouting, 'Shiiiiit!' Thankfully, someone pulled their car up sideways just before they got to the main road. It was a very lucky escape.

On another occasion, we thought it would be really fun to swap horses without actually getting off and touching the ground, like those horsey-acrobat types do. We were trotting down this hard road, which was quite stony, and tried to get our horses really close together, and when they were touching, I decided to go for it. I launched my top half over Poppy and my legs were behind me, still on Toddy. Letty, meanwhile, didn't move. The horses then very slowly started to edge apart and there was nothing I could do because I was staring at the floor, balanced across both of the horses, and Letty was just laughing. Inevitably, I landed flat on my back and was so winded I could barely breathe and didn't know whether to laugh or cry.

Letty's dad, Rick, gave us this beaten-up off-road car and we would spend hours driving around their massive farm. We would practise how to park and set each other courses around hay bales and markers, involving lots of twists, turns and some reversing. I remember one day I was driving towards the farm and I forgot to brake and crashed into this eighteenth-century wall attached to her family's house. I was terrified, but Rick was really cool about it.

By then, Dad had moved back to Mayfield in East Sussex, which was near St Bede's. One of our after-school activities was going skateboarding around the village, which sounds a bit bizarre, looking back. I said I was doing the activity but rather than skateboarding, I would go to his house and see him for half an hour. We would sit and chat, while Dad drank a cup of tea and I ate some sweets. Sometimes I would take my friends with me and he was always very welcoming to everyone. I never told my mum that I had seen him because I didn't want to upset her. Sometimes, when we'd a good chat or fun together, I felt torn.

In our car, Letty and I used to do stupid things, like pretend we were going off to meet our fake boyfriends, whom we called Ollie and Alex. Mine was Alex, which is a bit weird because I obviously started dating an Alex on the show. We used to talk about what we would do with them. Letty's giggle is really infectious and just makes me laugh more. I used to really fancy Letty's older brother, Miles, who was at Cirencester Agricultural College, and when he was at home he would take us out in his car to fêtes. Life outside of school was fun again. While I was fine at school, I was never studious because I knew it wouldn't really help me get better grades.

When I was fourteen, for New Year's Eve, we went to the house of some family friends called the Worssams, who were hosting a big party to celebrate. They were a lovely couple and they'd always stuck up for Mum when times were hard with Dad. Mum didn't want to go out because, since her split with Dad, she had put on quite a lot of weight and didn't feel very confident, but I insisted that we went and told her in no uncertain terms that no way was I staying home alone with her. So off we went and, as the evening wore on she was introduced to one of the Worssams' friends who she hadn't met before and they got on right from the start. She later said he was everything she could've wanted in a man. He was good-looking and a real gentleman. Mum said he seemed to know everyone and was funny, gentle and easy-going.

When I went inside, I saw her dancing with him and she was really smiling properly for the first time in what seemed like a long time. His name was Andrew and she told me a bit about him. I didn't want Mum to have a boyfriend because I was used to having her to myself and hated the

I didn't want Mum to have a boyfriend because I was used to having her to myself

idea of sharing her with someone. As far as I was concerned, life was finally steady and predictable again, so I was very apprehensive about having another man in our lives.

Andrew didn't call her for a few days after the party and when the phone finally did ring, on the fourth day, she was like a teenager again, all giggly and silly, and she said, 'Oh, Andrew, hiii!'

I thought, 'No way is this guy coming into our lives,' but slowly I started to see a change in her. She began to lose weight, did her nails again and took up smoking, which I hated, as did AL. She started to see more and more of him. I knew she was keen for Andrew and me to get on, and she used to do things like send him round to the stables to pick me up after I had been riding. I was always polite to his face, but secretly I just wanted it to be Mum and me at home, without any man in the middle.

One day, when they had been dating for a few months, Andrew came round to Lilac Cottage with his two daughters. He was a widower and had brought his two girls up alone, since they were aged seven and nine. Amanda was seventeen at the time and Minty was nineteen. I didn't want to meet the girls and was very reluctant to even come downstairs, but as we sat chatting round the fire in the sitting room, we hit it off immediately. Both girls are slim, blonde and cool, and Minty and I, in particular, really clicked because we are both Geminis. We talked about boys all the time. Minty was going out with this guitarist and they were really loved-up, but it didn't last very long. Amanda had a boyfriend at the time called Christian, who was blond, gorgeous and a bit hippyish; I used to really fancy him. We always laugh about the fact that when I later went off to board for my sixth-form years, I had a picture of him on my wall. They also got me into more modern music and, to this day, they send me tracks by cool new artists that I love. Ever since then, we have called each other sisters and they are like blood relatives to me.

I also remember thinking that Minty and Amanda were so cool because they smoked. Once, when I was in the car with Amanda and one of her friends, she offered me a cigarette and I started smoking it and felt so sick. I don't know why I continued to do it, but I don't smoke much. Sometimes when I was at home at Lilac Cottage with Letty, we would have a crafty cigarette in my room, which wasn't the easiest thing to do because the house was so old there were massive gaps under the doors, so you could hear and smell everything. We would lean as far as we could out of the window, puffing away. We used anything we could find to try to mask the smell, including hairspray, deodorant and candles. People used to come past the house and I didn't realise until recently that they used to tell my mum that we were smoking up there. At my Mum's birthday party at the end of last year, one of her friends came up to me and said, 'I used to see you and Letty leaning out the window smoking while was I walking the dogs. I always told your Mum.'

Mum used to pretend to be disapproving and would sniff the air and look appalled as she asked us if we had been smoking, but she was fairly relaxed and knew it was pretty standard teenage stuff.

Andrew and the girls had never been to Rock, so the following summer, Mum suggested that we rent a house there for all of us, including AL and Ollie. We had the best time ever, spending our days on the beach and the evenings at the house. Someone would bring out a guitar and we would all get very drunk, sing some tracks and party the night away. Minty and Amanda were the most brilliant company. We felt so complete as a family; we didn't need anyone else.

She took me to clubs like Boujis and Raffles in Chelsea, and to cool house parties

After that, I went to stay with Minty, who had moved to London, from time to time. She was living in a flat near Earl's Court and she took me to clubs like Boujis and Raffles in Chelsea, and to cool house parties, which were hosted by her friends. Everyone was really friendly towards me and I felt really grown-up. Also around then, Ollie started taking me out in Chelsea and Fulham. To make sure I got in to the clubs, he always asked one of his hot friends to put their arm around me, so I looked like I was his girlfriend. I used to think, 'Wow, he's got his arm around me. This is amazing.' I was so nervous about not getting past the door guy or girl, but Ollie seemed to know everyone and usually kissed him or her on both cheeks before we sailed straight in. We always had a table and there would always be drinks on ice in the middle. Everyone looked so glamorous and I found it really exciting.

Mum was very happy for me to go out with Minty and Ollie, even though I wasn't eighteen, because they would look out for me. Whenever Mum went to see Ollie, I would always go with her and we would go out and sometimes Mum would come too. I think, because I had been to so many schools, I was probably more mature than other girls my age and I looked older than I was, so Ollie and Minty's social circle didn't think I was too young and treated me as another friend. At school, I had often struggled to make connections with people, but in London I found it easy. I got along with everyone and was accepted for who I was immediately. It almost seemed like a secret set – and I was automatically part of it.

Also around this time, my brother started dating a gorgeous blonde TV presenter called Hannah Sandling and I really admired her. I would go and stay with him in his flat in London and Hannah would let me borrow her amazing clothes and took me to these big showbiz parties. All the photographers would be asking her to pose for them outside the various venues and on the red carpet and we would be momentarily blinded by the flash of their bulbs. It just felt really thrilling and I couldn't wait to leave school so I could live in London. Back at home, I used to play Stevie Wonder and George Michael's version of 'Living for the City' on repeat day after day and dream about all the parties I would go to and the fun I was going to have when I was finally old enough.

It almost seemed like a secret set and I was automatically part of it

At home, it was still strained, with Andrew round at Lilac Cottage all the time. He'd pretty much moved in with us by then, and I didn't like it. If the three of us were in the sitting room and Andrew got up and I sat where he had been, Mum used to say, 'Get out of Andrew's chair.' It used to make me so mad, as I felt that it was my home, not his. Occasionally, if he was being ballsy, he would tell me to be nice to Mum and I would reply, 'Don't tell me what to do'. Ollie and I really tested him. I remember, on one of Ollie's birthdays, we all had dinner at the Big Easy, a restaurant on the King's Road, and Ollie stripped off all his clothes and started dancing naked on the table, to see Andrew's reaction, but he just laughed. On another occasion, when we all went skiing together, I wrote something rude on the bonnet of his car in the snow, but again he took it really well. Little things really annoyed me about him being around, but I was happy with my new sisters, Minty and Amanda, so I was willing to try to forget the things I didn't like.

I think having the girls around made me grow up quite quickly because they had a huge input into my teenage life. They would always dress me up and were slowly teaching me all the things I wanted to know about relationships, make-up and fashion. With Ollie around less and less, Minty and Amanda became my new idols and I really looked up to them.

Mum also loved the girls as if they were her own. They really took to her, after not having a mother figure in their lives for a long time, and Mum gave them advice and did a lot of things for them. Minty moved in with Mum for a while when she was looking for work and later was a stand-in mother of the bride at her wedding in 2012. Mum and Andrew's relationship didn't work out in the end, for many reasons, but we still consider their romance and our meeting the girls the hugest bolt of good luck for us.

In the summer of 2006, I sat my GCSEs. I hated exams so much, especially maths, and I would just sit and write random numbers on the pages, so it looked like I had actually looked through the paper and thought about answering some of the questions. I always had extra time because of my learning difficulty, which was even worse, because five minutes in, I had nothing to write. I had no idea in the slightest what they were asking me to do, even when it came to the most basic of tasks. English wasn't so bad because I loved writing stories and it was one of my favourite things to do when I was younger. I also quite enjoyed biology. If I actually understood something in one of my biology lessons, like how a certain part of the body worked, I would feel so chuffed with myself and would take so much care over my homework, writing with my best handwriting. I loved art too, but mostly, I think I was a bit of a lost cause. Predictably, my GCSE results weren't great, but I'd had no expectations. Mum didn't mind; we knew I was never going be a brain surgeon and, because of her upbringing, where education wasn't considered paramount, she never put pressure on me to do better. In the summer after my GCSEs, I started doing a few odd jobs, working in local pubs in the area, serving drinks behind the bar or waitressing, to earn some pocket money. I never stuck to anything for that long, but enjoyed the company and the work.

We were undecided about whether I should go on to do my A-Levels and, for a few weeks that summer, we looked into other options for me, such as secretarial courses in London or becoming a nanny, because I love children. For a long time, we couldn't make a decision about what the best course of action would be, but in the end it was Andrew who suggested to Mum that I go to a boarding school for my final two years of school, because I was still so young. When Mum decided that I was definitely going back to school, I was a bit angry, because my friends were really envious of the fact that potentially school would be a thing of the past for me. Also, I felt that Andrew was trying to get me out of the way at home so that he could have Mum all to himself. Deep down though, I knew it was the right thing to do, so I'm glad he did say something to Mum and that I did do my A-Levels.

My final school was Taunton School in Somerset, where I went to study photography, art and leisure and recreation for my A-Levels. As we drove up the long drive towards the beautiful old buildings, it was like being transported to Harry Potter's Hogwarts. There were good-looking boys at every turn, which peaked my interest even more. Looking back, I feel so privileged to have gone to so many wonderful schools. For a long time, I took it for granted, but after my different experiences, I appreciate how lucky I have been.

Before I boarded properly, the school wanted me to stay overnight, so they could get to know me a little better and make sure I would behave. In the boarding house, I talked to the other girls about all the clubs that Ollie and Minty had taken me to and I felt like I fitted in well.

When I moved in for good, I packed up a trunk AL had given me with all my stuff and Andrew drove the three of us down to Taunton. Knowing I wouldn't see Mum for weeks and weeks, we both cried in the car for four hours non-stop. I was very lucky, as I was given my own room and many of the girls had to share. Mum came in and gave the room what I call the 'mummy touch' by making it really homely and making up my bed for me, and she helped me put up some pictures, but saying goodbye was heart-breaking. She sobbed all the way home and then endlessly for days. This time round, I recovered far quicker, but we missed each other terribly.

The housemaster and mistress, who were called Mr and Mrs Hallows, took me under their wing and gave me tea and talked to me about how it would get easier after a few weeks. I had befriended a girl called Kat during my previous overnight stay and we stuck together in the first few days. She was from Bath and was really intelligent and sporty and had these big eyes, like Bambi. I remember, on the first evening, we sat on the steps of one of the games huts and I said to her that we should go back there on the last night, after we had completed our two years – and we did. There was a real feeling of community there and I felt accepted. It was like one big family and everyone looked out for each other. I got loads of individual attention from the teachers and there were always people to go to if I needed help with my work. It didn't matter that I wasn't the best at anything.

One of the highlights of our first few weeks was receiving post from our family and friends in our pigeonholes. One day a big package arrived for me and I was so excited. I ripped it apart and Minty had sent me loads of pictures in a big envelope of our holidays and the fun we used to have together and I put them up all around my room. Mum would send me silly pictures and drawings saying, 'I love you and I miss you.' I found it really hard at first, but as the weeks ticked past it got easier.

Soon boarding became a way of life. There were loads of activities every day, like quiz and karaoke nights and pizza evenings. I remember once being in the boarding house, when we were all watching television, and I said that I'd love to be

I loved the idea of being in London and being invited to all the best parties and walking down the red carpets on the TV. It's something I had thought for a while, especially after I'd spent some time with my brother's girlfriend, Hannah. There wasn't anyone in particular that I wanted to be like, but I loved the idea of being in London and being invited to all the best parties and walking down the red carpets. When I told the others my thoughts, they all looked horrified and said stuff like, 'No way. Why would you want to do that? I'd hate to be on TV.' From then on, I kept my thoughts to myself about what I wanted for my future. I think a lot of girls would secretly love to be on TV, whether they admit it or not.

From childhood, whenever anyone asked me what I wanted to do after school, I would always trot out the same line: 'I want to live a spontaneous life.' I think that was Ba Ba's influence on me. I loved the idea of being a singer and, while I definitely wasn't tone deaf – I sounded brilliant in the shower – I was far too nervous to sing in front of a huge crowd, so you would never have found me queuing to audition in front of Simon Cowell! I also thought the world of modelling sounded so glamorous, but I was never told that I was pretty. I could eat for England and I didn't really take care of my appearance, so I never thought about that as an option.

While I was at Taunton, Mum rented out Lilac Cottage, moved to London and took a year's rental on a flat before she found somewhere to buy in Fulham. I loved going to stay at the London flat because Ollie, AL, Minty and Amanda were living nearby and it felt like home. I had always dreamed of being in London when I finished school and with my Mum already living there, I knew it would make it easier for me to make the transition, once I had finished my A-Levels. It was an exciting new chapter in all of our lives.

I used to hate Sunday nights, when I had to go back to school, after staying in London for the weekend. Mum would cook a massive roast with all the trimmings for Ollie, AL, Andrew, Minty, Amanda and me and, afterwards, I would have to get the tube to Paddington, with my enormous Jack Wills bag slung over my shoulder, and make the three-hour train journey back to Somerset. When I arrived back at Taunton station it would always be really late and I would often walk back to school in the dark. I used to tell myself it was only for a few more months and then my life in London would start in earnest.

When I finally left Taunton, I knew I would be OK, but I didn't have a clue which direction I would go in. All my friends were going to university and were meeting boys and having fun, but we knew that further education wasn't for me and that I'd probably end up spending too much money and dropping out, like Ollie, so we knew that was definitely not an option. I felt a bit bereft, as I had no idea what I would do. By then, Mum had bought a small two-bedroom house on Crookham Road in Parsons Green and I moved in with her.

Mum and I started to think about what I could do for work and AL helped me write my CV. We talked about the possibility of working abroad for a year, taking a nanny job or even doing a ski season in one of the resorts we had visited on holiday. Then AL had a brainwave and put a tongue-in-cheek post on Facebook, selling my talents to her group of friends in London. She said I was not the most organised person in the world and that I was a little bit naughty and not always on time, but that I was a hard worker and lots of fun to have around. One of her friends replied and said they knew there was a receptionist job going at the offices of the luxury property development company Candy & Candy. I had a bit of a head start

I told her I wanted to be a celebrity!

because both Ollie and AL knew the Candy brothers, Nick and Christian, so I crossed my fingers and hoped for the best. It was the first job interview I had ever had and I wasn't sure what to expect, but I got on very well with both brothers and I was offered the job. When Amy, the girl who later became my boss, asked me what I wanted to do, apparently I told her I wanted to be a celebrity!

The Candy & Candy offices were incredible. Being a property and interior design company, the London headquarters were an advert for their work. Everything was black, shiny and modern. There were six of us manning two reception desks: one on the ground floor and the other on the first floor. We used to have to wear black dresses and high heels and have immaculate hair and make-up. I was always disastrous at that – my hair would be disgusting and my tights always had holes in them. My nails would always be a bit manky and Amy would make me hold out my hands for inspection. She would go through each sorry finger and say, 'Fail, fail, fail, borderline pass, fail.' She was half-joking, but often she would tell me she would send me home if I wore another slouchy jumper-dress with UGG boots. She tried to be cross with me, but she could never keep a serious face and we always ended up giggling when I did something wrong. If a siren went past outside and she and I were on different desks, we used to ring each other and say, 'It's the fashion police for you!'

We started socialising together outside of work and I took her to the Duke on the Green in Parsons Green every Thursday night, which we nicknamed 'thirsty Thursdays', and we hung out with my brother and his friends, so at times it was hard to have a professional relationship. She had to tell me off if I had done something wrong, but it was difficult if we'd been out drinking the night before. We often ended our drinking sessions by going back to someone's house, where we played drinking games that involved doing handstands up against the wall and the splits, and the boys daring each other to run across the road naked.

I don't think I was the best receptionist. All the other girls on reception were really preened and they nicknamed me 'Naughty Lexi'. The fact that the brothers are so successful and are worth so much money went straight over my head and I treated them like I treat anyone else and used to send stupid emails to Nick. I managed to get away with quite a lot and was often hungover and tired. Most of the time, it was incredibly busy, with the phones ringing off the hook, so it could be really stressful. I got used to people calling and pretending they knew Nick or Christian, often trying to sell them something. They were often arrogant and I learned to be quite short, but polite. I used to take down a lot of messages, but my handwriting was illegible and, most of the time, I wasn't able to read it back afterwards.

There was also a very complex system of signing people in and out, with these electronic passes, and around this time there were always contractors and agents coming in to discuss the big Candy & Candy development One Hyde Park. We always had to keep our cool, whatever the situation. There was one particularly hectic Monday morning when the sound system went crazy and was so loud we could barely hear ourselves think, but we had to pretend everything was fine and smile sweetly at all the visitors who were coming in and out of the building.

One day Nick and Christian told me we had a really important client coming in and, sure enough, this very smart guy walked into the reception and I took his jacket from him and they all went off into a meeting room together. An hour or so later, the brothers came down and asked me to get the man's coat and I couldn't remember which one it was, so I just said, 'I really don't recognise your coat. Perhaps you could check inside the coat cupboard yourself.' And then I added, 'You never know, you might choose a better one.' It wasn't my finest moment!

Amy realised that one of my strengths was organising extracurricular fun for the staff, so I was in charge of planning events for us, like rounders, a BBQ (of course, it chucked it down with rain) or karaoke, and I was always the first to make a complete idiot of myself. When they opened the Candy Bar and it was the first night, Amy and I and a couple of the other girls decided to show our faces. I had a massive crush on one of the design assistants who had been working on the bar, which had developed over weeks into a small obsession. I was crazy about him. Attempting to style it out, I went outside for a cigarette in my UGG boots, which I would have lived in if I was allowed to, and afterwards, when I was walking across the stone floors of the reception back towards the bar, I completely stacked it. I was mortified that anyone at all, especially the guy in question, might have seen me sprawled across the floor. Luckily, only Amy and a couple of others had witnessed the calamity, but they took great delight replaying it over and over on the CCTV system, which is what I did constantly when other people fell over.

When Mum sold the house on Crookham Road, I needed to find somewhere to live and my friend Harry told me that a girl he knew called Kate was looking for someone to share her home on Bishop's Road, which was around the corner. It was there that I met Francesca 'Cheska' Hull. Like me, she wasn't your typical Chelsea girl. Her family comes from Salcombe in Devon, where her mother runs a upmarket fashion boutique called Amelia's Attic, and Cheska grew up there. She won a scholarship to St Mary's boarding school in Wantage, Oxfordshire, and went on to study fashion promotion at the University for the Creative Arts at Farnham in Surrey. She worked hard, but also played hard and by the time I met her, she was working for a corporate events company, getting into the office at 7.30 a.m. and often staying until 11 p.m., organising events. She was also writing a 'Girl About Town' column for *Matchbox*, a glossy magazine that went out in Notting Hill, Knightsbridge and Kensington and Chelsea. There were always loads of boys in her life and, like me, life was all about having fun.

As I mentioned before, Cheska and I were really naughty and we'd go out all the time and would sometimes wake up Kate, whom we called Square, when we came in. Square would often send us really

Cheska and I were really naughty and we'd go out all the time

angry emails saying 'Why did you do x, y or z? I'm not happy at all about it!' There was only one occasion I can remember that we managed to get Square drunk and keep her up late to have fun. Mostly she was in bed at 9 p.m. with a good book and cup of hot chocolate. Cheska and I couldn't have been more different to her.

But most of the time, Square wasn't much fun to live with. One time she accused Cheska and I of pooing on her carpet – seriously – apparently there was actually a human poo in her bedroom! In the morning, when Cheska was making herself some breakfast in the kitchen after a big night out, Square asked, 'Did you or Binky poo on my carpet?'

'Absolutely not. Why on earth would we do that?' Cheska replied. She was appalled and really angry – I mean, who on earth poos on the carpet? I was equally pissed off when she relayed the story, although we did laugh about it afterwards.

To cut a long story short, it turns out it was actually one of Square's friends who'd pooed on the carpet, which we discovered when we found a pair of Kate's pooey tracksuit bottoms that the friend – who had been very drunk – had been wearing, but they had denied being the culprit. Kate never apologised and, after a while, Cheska couldn't handle her and left but I stayed for a time.

After two years with Candy & Candy, I interned at another company called Lionsgate on Berkeley Square for a brief time. It was 2010, the year before *Made in Chelsea* started. Cheska had been approached about an MTV show called *Super Sweet World Class*. It was like *My Super Sweet 16* but for older kids and not quite so bratty. They asked her to throw a lavish party for hundreds of people and she asked me if I wanted to be involved. I told her there was absolutely no way I would do it on my own. 'If I'm doing it, you're doing it with me,' I told her and we agreed to face the challenge together.

We were interviewed by the production team about our lives in Chelsea and got the job. We were really delighted. We ended up spending six full days filming, as we planned a party with a vintage-Hollywood theme, which was held at the trendy Shoreditch bar McQueen. I'm not very good at talking to camera, but I didn't mind it when they filmed me messing about, and I found the whole experience really enjoyable. We dressed the walls of the bar up with life-size pictures of ourselves dressed up as Hollywood icons Audrey Hepburn and Marilyn Monroe, and this celebrity stylist, Giles Pearson, who had worked with people like Lady Gaga and Beyoncé, helped us style ourselves for the shoot. I wore a little black dress, long gloves and pearls, with my hair up, as Audrey and Cheska looked amazing in this white dress and a blonde wig as Marilyn. It was quite tongue-in-cheek, but the resulting pictures were perfect.

I'm not very good at talking to camera, but I didn't mind it when they filmed me messing about

On the night itself we arrived at the event in the back of a vintage American convertible. The lighting was provided by the company that illuminates the stars when they arrive on the red carpet at the Oscars, and guests were greeted by gorgeous guys wearing almost nothing but gold spray paint. As the party got underway, we performed a burlesque dance as showgirls, with these huge black-feathered fans, which we had been taught by a top choreographer. I did freak out beforehand, as I kept forgetting the routine, and we were shaking with nerves. It was such an adrenalin rush, but went really well in the end.

Seeing myself on-screen for the first time was really surreal

We watched the final show when it aired on MTV in a bar in Shoreditch, with all our friends and family. Seeing myself on-screen for the first time was really surreal, but we all got quite drunk, which helped ease my nerves. I think I came across as the really ditsy one, and while Cheska would be rushing about organising everything, I was just drinking champagne in the hot tub. I was totally myself. While Cheska did do the lion's share of the hard work, I made up for it by buying her a diamond and ruby encrusted ring which was once worn by Sienna Miller, so she didn't stay mad at me for long.

After the adrenalin rush of the filming and the run-up to the show, I almost felt a bit depressed going back to my job and then out in the evenings like before. Ordinary day-to-day life seemed boring in comparison to what we had just been through. Mum assured me that I would soon get over it and, after a while, life would return to normal, but I longed for the buzz of being on camera and the excitement and anticipation of watching the show after the cameras had stopped rolling.

Not long after that, I got a job as a receptionist for a hedge-fund company called LingBridge, which was run by these two guys, Gopi and Bridgey. Bridgey was a hilarious party animal with ginger hair and made me laugh a lot. It turns out I got the job because he thought I would bring entertainment value to the office. In my interview, he asked me what I thought of Bloomberg.

'It's really pretty. It's a flower, isn't it?' I said.

'Erm, no, it's that machine over there. Right, you're hired.'

Again, I don't think I was a particularly good receptionist and couldn't really be trusted to do what I was asked. On one occasion, they left me in charge and told me to sell some shares and, as they were walking in, I was buying them and they were shouting, 'Noooo, you're supposed to be selling!' Clearly I wasn't cut out for the world of finance!

My top Chelsea hangouts

I love living in Chelsea and there are loads of places I would recommend for drinks, dinner, a night out or a daytime treat. Here are my top picks:

♛ Bluebird, 350 King's Road, London, SW3 5UU (www.bluebird-restaurant.co.uk).

I love the Bluebird because it's got a really great courtyard area outside, which is fantastic in the summer. The restaurant serves great food and champagne – and the prices are reasonable. There is also a bar, food and wine store and bakery in the basement. It's right in the middle of the King's Road, so is in the heart of the action and a real celeb-magnet.

➡

Maggie's, 329 Fulham Road, London, SW10 9QL
(www.maggies-club.com).

My friend owns this club, which is named after
Maggie Thatcher. It's really wacky and fun, with
80s-inspired retro décor, like tables shaped like
Rubik's Cubes. It also serves kitsch cocktails and
the waiters are like Tom Cruise in *Cocktail*. The DJs
always play my favourite 80s tracks and I feel like I
know every song off by heart. I always have a good
night when I go there.

 Raffles, 287 King's Road, London, SW3 5EW
(www.raffleschelsea.com).

This is where I first discovered nightlife in Chelsea
and my stepsister Minty does the PR there, so
whenever I pop in, there are always people there that
I know and everyone is always looking glam. They
have had many A-list and royal guests, including the
Queen, who visited back in the 70s. In 2012 they
had a launch for new members and people like David
Gandy and Paloma Faith came along to celebrate.
There is a podium there that I always dance on when
I'm drunk. I think I might own it!

 Geales, 1 Cale Street, London, SW3 3QT
(www.geales.com).

This is a fantastic, posh, fish and chips restaurant on Chelsea Green. Loads of top celebrities like Kylie Minogue go there and it's really relaxed and serves the best comfort food in London.

♕ Big Easy, 332–334 King's Road, London, SW3 5UR (www.bigeasy.co.uk).

I adore this American-style diner for the great food and buzzing atmosphere. The vast menu ranges from sizzling fajitas to racks of smoked baby back ribs, slathered in their house sauce, and massive lobsters. The portions are astronomical, so make sure you arrive hungry. If you have space for dessert, there are glorious diner classics, like red velvet and carrot cake. As well as good food, the music is always great and they often have a live band downstairs. My family and I have celebrated loads of birthdays here and it's always really fun.

♕ The White Horse, 1–3 Parsons Green, London, SW6, 4UL (www.whitehorsesw6.com).

Situated on the corner of Parsons Green, we all call this pub 'the Sloaney Pony' and I am always guaranteed to see people that I know there. It's a lovely place to go for a relaxed drink and, when the sun is shining, it has a great beer garden at the back.

👑 Boma Bar & Restaurant, 116 Wandsworth Bridge Road, London, SW6 2TF (www.bomas.co.uk).

I used to go to this first-class restaurant all the time because some of my friends own it. Don't be fooled by the basic décor: the menu is great and they do fabulous breakfasts, which accompany their Elderflower Bellinis perfectly. The Sunday roasts are delicious alongside one of their killer Bloody Marys.

👑 The Ship, 41 Jews Row, Wandsworth, London, SW18 1TB (www.theship.co.uk).

Right on the bank on the River Thames, this pub is always packed. It hosts loads of regular events, like live music nights on Sundays and Tuesdays, and it has a cool beer garden.

👑 The Phene, 9 Phene Street, London, SW3 5NY (www.thephene.com).

A favourite with my *Made in Chelsea* cast mates, this venue has a traditional saloon bar, a conservatory restaurant and a more private lounge area on the first floor.

👑 JuJu, 316–318 King's Road, London, SW3 5UH (www.jujulondon.com).

Another great drinking establishment which has

the most immense cocktail list. I try to avoid drinking cocktails, as I can't really handle them, but I'm told the signature Chelsea Ice Teas and the Pornstar Martinis are great, if a little pricey. Gabby had a birthday party here not long after *Made in Chelsea* started filming and performed some of her own tracks.

 Love Bakery, 319 King's Road, London, SW3 5EP (www.lovebakery.co.uk).

Mark-Francis may claim that Chelsea girls don't eat, but clearly this one does. I'm not crazy about sweet treats, but if they are your thing, Love Bakery is the perfect place to go for a sugar fix. They serve cupcakes and cookies by the dozen and are always creating loads of new flavours according to the season, but also sell old favourites like red velvet, vanilla and lemon and rose. Rosie loves it so much, she can often be found behind the counter!

 The Brown Cow, 676 Fulham Road, London, SW6 5SA (www.thebrowncowpub.co.uk).

This pub is dog friendly and just round the corner from my house, so I love taking Scrumble with me for brunch or a roast at the weekends. Prince Harry was spotted here last year, after the Remembrance Sunday service at the Cenotaph.

7

DID CHARLES DICKENS WRITE *WINNIE THE POOH*?

People always ask me if *Made in Chelsea* is scripted and the answer is definitely no. There are no actors, scripts or rehearsals; I would be completely hopeless at learning lines anyway. It is about real people and real relationships, but I guess situations are put under the magnifying glass, so romances move a lot quicker than they might do in ordinary life.

People always ask me if Made in Chelsea is scripted and the answer is definitely no

The filming process started in February 2011 and I still had no idea what to expect. I didn't want too many people to know about the show because I thought they would try to find fault with it or that if it didn't happen I would look stupid, so I shared the news with a bare minimum of people in my life. My mum was so supportive from day one – and was really excited and happy for me – and AL quickly came round to the idea, but Ollie, Minty, Amanda and Andrew hated the idea of it and tried to stop me from getting involved. I suspected they had reservations for different reasons. Ollie was very established in Chelsea by that time and a lot of his friends wouldn't dream of taking part in a show like *Made in Chelsea*. He didn't think it was the right thing to do, but I'm not classy so I didn't care! He wrote me long, pleading emails and messages every day about how it was a bad decision and how I would end up looking stupid. Ollie even suggested to Mum that we have a family meeting, but Mum could see what a good opportunity it was and I always listened to her. If she hadn't urged me to do it, even though I really wanted to, I think I may have bowed down to the pressure, but I think she could see how lucky I was to have made it onto the final cast list.

Minty, Amanda and Andrew also got quite annoyed with me when I decided to go for it. Andrew was just really sticky about it and hated the thought of me being in a reality show, full stop. Minty didn't speak to me for a few weeks, but eventually, after a complete stand-off, she realised that I wouldn't change because of it and told me she was sorry if I thought she wasn't being supportive.

Of course it bothered me that so many important people in my life weren't encouraging me and while my attitude was still 'I'll do what I want' to everyone else, underneath I was very sensitive and apprehensive about it. Regardless, my overriding feeling about it was a good one, although I genuinely thought it would be a one-series thing that a few people would watch and then forget about.

When the first series started filming, Ollie Locke and Gabriella Ellis had only just started dating. I had initially met Gabby at the *Super Sweet World Class* party, but I didn't speak to her for very long that night, so I only really started to get to know her when she and Ollie began dating. I didn't want to like her because I thought she would take Ollie away from me. Of course she is great and we got on really well, because she is so outgoing and fun. Ollie had asked her to take part in the show with him and she'd agreed. She's a musician and had already had a number one single in her native Greece and had sold thousands of records, so she hoped it would be good exposure for her music.

The first time we did any filming we were in a restaurant, drinking champagne. I was with Ollie and Cheska. By that point, Ollie and I were really close. He had taken me down to Southampton, where he grew up, and we had gone on a boat-trip with some of his friends. Back then, we saw each other every day, because we lived so close. Cheska worked hard at work and didn't always want to be hungover and because Ollie was doing club promoting, he was a bit freer, and I was always happy to keep him company and go out at a moment's notice. We were – and still are – very much on the same wavelength. We had similar upbringings in the sense that while we both went to amazing schools and were really lucky, I don't think we fitted into the trust-fund stereotype that many of our fellow cast mates did. He even says that when he was younger, working in nightclubs, he used to clean up other people's vomit; now that's something I'd love to see!

The next time we were filmed was when we were at Lilac

Cottage, in the sitting room, in front of the log fire. After Mum sold the house on Crookham Road, she eventually moved back to Sussex. We had broken down on the motorway on our trip from London to Sussex because Ollie had forgotten to put petrol in his car – stupid boy! We were so nervous and had sat on the side of the motorway, all windswept and stressed, until we were rescued and eventually made it with seconds to spare before they wanted to start.

The three of us sat around the fire and talked about how great it was to get out of London and into the country, and Ollie declared that he 'loved the smell of cow shit'. By that point, Ollie, Cheska and I were such close *I was still really self-conscious* friends, and that made things a bit easier, but I was still really self-conscious.

Then we sat around the table in the kitchen, while cooking roast chicken, and talked about Ollie's date with Gabriella and Cheska's new blogging job for *Matchbox*. By that point, I don't think things between Ollie and Gabriella were that good, because they had been spending so much time together and it had been moving too quickly. She totally adored him, so I felt really bad about it, but there was nothing that I could do. Ollie was nervous that it was going to unravel. I think he hoped the experience of being on the show together would bring them closer and iron out any problems that they had.

Our next big occasion was the Raffles party for socialite Amber Atherton's jewellery launch. Again, I was really nervous and had no idea what to expect. Spencer Matthews was there; I had met him when we had been briefly introduced a long time before, on a night out. I saw Caggie Dunlop and Millie Mackintosh as they were walking in and said hello. I had also met Hugo Taylor a week before, in the club Embargo, on the King's Road. I was with Cheska and she had pointed him out and said he had been quite rude to her when they had met, but I went and introduced myself and he was polite to me. We were all in our separate groups and didn't interact for a while. Caggie and I later became quite friendly. She is a really great girl and gives very sound advice.

Cheska and I sat down at a table with Mark-Francis and his friend Gabilicious, while they talked about Topshop being a complete turn-off – and it's still my favourite store! When I said I wanted to order some food, Mark-Francis made that comment: 'Chelsea girls don't eat.'

'Chelsea girls don't eat'

When I replied, 'This one does,' he shot back, 'Well, hence the cellulite.' I burst into tears and ran out. Everyone was telling me it was fine, but I was so worried that everyone would think I was really fat. Nobody wanted anyone to say anything bad about them and I was anxious about how I would come across on screen. I was just really embarrassed and also thought he wasn't very funny. I didn't warm to Mark-Francis initially, and didn't really understand his humour, but now I know him better, I love him – he's one of a kind and, despite that first impression, he's a real old-school gentleman. It turned out that Gabilicious was really nice too.

After the Raffles event the three of us went out for some drinks afterwards. We wondered what people would think of us and were completely clueless about how popular the show might be.

Months later, we watched the first show as a group. Everyone was there with their little groups of friends and family. I took my mum and my friend Lulu. We all went out beforehand for a few drinks because I was so nervous. By then, I was dating a guy called Charlie and was so into him and was really happy. Watching myself felt very surreal and I hated the way my voice sounded and how I looked. The whole evening was just weird. In the first show, Rosie and Amber were particularly nasty about Cheska and her 'Girl About Town' blog, saying it had 'potential to be quite offensive'. Cheska was a bit miffed, but she didn't let on that the comments had bothered her. They were also quite mean about our clothes. I didn't really care about what they had said; it didn't upset me. I think Rosie felt a bit embarrassed. I know her really well now and she's not like that. I think maybe they were just trying to make an impact. Sometimes, watching the show can be quite cringeworthy. Luckily I'm not one of the bitchy ones, but watching someone slagging off someone else who is just behind them can be a bit awkward, to say the least.

When we travelled to Chamonix in the Alps this was filmed for the show, which was so exciting. It was very last-minute. The morning we had to leave, I was so hungover, because we had been out the night before; I actually jumped into the shower with Cheska, while she was yelling at me to get out. We put our favourite onesies on and we went on our own to the airport and then waited in a bar for ages to be picked up. Ollie and Gabriella had organised a romantic ski trip together, but we knew Ollie had wanted us to go with him. We were nervous about Gabby's reaction and hoped she wouldn't be pissed off when we turned up. As it turns out, I do think she was excited to see us, although she was probably also a bit annoyed that we had gatecrashed their trip.

When we jumped into the hot tub with them, I left my towel on until the very last minute, in the hope that there wouldn't be too much flesh on show. I was actually so excited to be there with my best friends that I fell out of the jacuzzi backwards.

I know everyone thought Ollie's neon all-in-one ski suit was hilarious, but by then, I was used to his mad fashions, like his famous Union Jack trousers, his surfer shorts and his massive hoodies. He loves his make-up and always has his eyelash curlers and Touche Éclat to hand. Getting ready for a night out with him is like getting ready for a night out with one of my female friends. As I said before, I always had an inkling he was bisexual, but he genuinely hadn't told many people and his mum, Sarah, was still in the dark about his sexuality.

When we were in Chamonix I was single and I hadn't properly got over my ex, Simon. I was just sitting on the snowy mountainside just chilling with the others when I caught his eye. When he said 'Hello Alex' and I realised it was him, I was floored. I ran off camera. I felt quite excited because I still really liked him. He had just been on a boys' holiday to Egypt and got mugged on the way to the airport and had his money and phone stolen, so I don't know how he made it to Chamonix. He had a girlfriend at the time, who knew about me and my history with Simon and she was quite wary. He hadn't told her about the trip and after the episode aired on

TV, I think it's safe to say she wasn't best pleased and she dropped off all his belongings at his flat the next day.

I wanted to know if he still wanted to be with me, because I wanted to understand his motives for being on the show

After I'd recovered from the shock and excitement of seeing Simon, I was actually a bit miffed. We went off to a bar together and talked more about our relationship and why it hadn't worked out. I wanted to know if he still wanted to be with me, because I wanted to understand his motives for being on the show. I had suppressed my feelings for him for such a long time, but when we were hanging out just the two of us, laughing and chatting, all the emotions came flooding back. I think he felt nervous talking to me about it.

When we got back to the chalet for Ollie's birthday dinner, which was being made by this incredible chef, it was quite awkward, because I didn't want Simon to be embarrassed when the others threw questions at him about what was going on between us. We all got really drunk in the chalet and were up dancing for ages in the living area. Unfortunately, Simon was going back to Egypt the next day to continue with his holiday there, so had to go back to his hotel room, rather than stay over in our chalet. In many ways, I wished I hadn't seen him and I felt a bit sad because it was as if we had ended the relationship all over again.

The next day I told him exactly how I felt and that he needed to dump his girlfriend, because he always came running back. I felt he had screwed me over in the past, and I don't think he could really believe what I was saying, because I was so brutal. For a while, after that trip, he tried to get me back and was constantly calling and texting, but I knew that it would just go back to how it was before and we would split up and then get back together again. It just wasn't meant to be, and I knew that.

I also knew that Ollie was going to split up with Gabriella, and I felt awful. That trip felt a bit like the beginning of the end. He told me that he had dated guys in the past and I knew what a big deal it was to share the news with not only his family and friends, but also people who would be watching the show. I thought it was brilliant that he had come out – what a way to do it! I loved the fact that he could joke that my new 'bi best friend' was 'the cheap equivalent of a gay best friend'. I love Ollie and everything about him, so it was never going to bother me. In fact, I think the experience made us closer.

As a group we had attended a charity auction on HMS *President*. I was nervous because I knew Ollie was going to split up with Gabby and it's awful being dumped, full stop, let alone when the whole world is watching. I was tired and hadn't made a huge effort with my clothes and make-up. The other girls, like Millie and Rosie, always looked amazing and we weren't as stylish and cool as them but I think our story-lines brought something totally different to the show – a much more fun vibe. I was happy with my gang and couldn't really be bothered to make an effort to get to know the others better, so again, we kept ourselves to ourselves. Of course, I've got to know some of them really well and, these days, I count many of them as really good friends.

After Ollie broke the news to Gabriella that their romance was over, I was really caught in the middle. Ollie was one of my closest best friends, but I also did my best for Gabriella and spent a lot of time on the phone, trying to counsel her through it and being a shoulder to cry on. Sometimes she would come and stay with me overnight if she was particularly upset. I didn't want to take sides, but because she was a girl, I felt for her and understood what she was going through. I think she and I got a lot closer at that time.

There are some times back then where Cheska and I look bright orange because we had overdone it with the fake tan the night before, because we knew we were going to be wearing skimpy tops. By that point, it was summer and I was with my boyfriend Charlie and was totally loved-up. We were really into each other and were going out loads. I remember never wanting to leave him. I was so in love with him that I resented the time I had away from him. I was also still working at LingBridge, so when I did have time with him, it was really precious.

One of my favourite times from that series was when Ollie went on a date with Matt Aiden, the guy that he met in the park, and we were at his house, listening in to the date via the phone. Cheska and I had a few drinks and we were trying on his clothes, lots of which were decidedly unisex.

The most bonkers moment from the first series was when Fredrik Ferrier sang opera at the masquerade ball. He sounded great, but I couldn't help but laugh at how OTT it was. Good on him for learning how to sing that though. It just showed how different I was from most of the other cast

It just showed how different I was from most of the other cast members

members. I can't say that opera has featured very heavily in my life so far!

By the end of the first series I was spending as much time as I could with Charlie and I was involved in the show but Mum still wouldn't let me give up my job at LingBridge and I was struggling to keep everything afloat. I'm quite proud of myself for holding on to the job for as long as I did because it would've been much simpler for me to pack it in long before I did.

Before the show even launched on TV, it was getting quite a lot of hype and great reviews, with Digital Spy saying, 'It's all incredibly silly, but we're already falling in love with it a little bit and it will fill a lovely *TOWIE* shaped hole for the summer.' And Heatworld declared: 'We never thought we'd ever find reality/staged drama TV love again after *TOWIE* but *Made in Chelsea* has sucked us deep into its self-obsessed vortex and we're loving every minute of it!' Praise indeed. We were delighted with the early responses to the show; they were better than I had ever hoped for.

The show first aired on 9 May 2011. I got lots of text messages from friends saying 'well done' and lots of people I hadn't spoken to for a very long time came out of the woodwork. One of the girls who had bullied me at St Mary's even texted to tell me she was 'proud' of me, which was a bit strange. I quickly had to change my settings on Facebook, as lots of random people started friend-requesting me, and I was just starting to get to grips with Twitter, which is the way I talk

Mum posing with AL just after I was born at The Portland Hospital

Me and AL staring each other out

From the beginning, I adored my brother Ollie

I have always been naughty, hence the nickname 'Binky'

Ba Ba and Cliffy, my wonderful grandparents

Mummy and Daddy at their wedding at Chelsea Register Office

My first
horse-riding
lesson, aged just
six months

Letty and I loved
Pony Club Camp

I have always loved riding and am pretty fearless

When we were hungry daddy took a photograph

This picture is from one of my school diaries, which AL probably helped with

My first school photograph at St Bede's – I think it's safe to say my looks have improved over the years!

With Mum, AL and Ollie on another one of our wonderful holidays

A more recent picture of Mum, Ollie, AL and me on a night out

About to go out partying with my big sis

My life in London has always been about having as much fun as possible

Hanging out in Sussex with my friends from home

Lucy and I have become good friends since being on the show together

Cheska, Ollie and I have always been close

In a 'kiss' sandwich at an event with Spencer and Jamie

On the front row at London Fashion Week with Louise and Mark-Francis

Winning the BAFTA – a very proud moment for the *MIC* team

I've become a bit more relaxed on the red carpet over the past few years

Appearing on *Jonathan Ross* with Jamie, Spencer, Ollie and Millie, another real highlight

With Alex and Lucy on a night out

For a long time things
with Alex were great

For Christmas Alex
bought me a holiday to
Goa – it was glorious!

to fans of the show now. Lots of people were saying we were the posh version of *TOWIE* and we were automatically pitted against them in the headlines, but I never saw it like that.

The launch show pulled in 510,000 viewers, which was a blinding start. Twitter also went crazy and it was in one of the top trending positions for ages. I was really surprised that people enjoyed it so much, but I guess it features stuff we can all relate to – love, friendship and fun. And while most people don't have the lifestyle that most of the show's stars have, people told me they loved the fact that they could relate to our struggles and the changing and growing we were all going through, and they enjoyed the fact that we appeared to not give a shit. The fans also found the ongoing romances compelling.

Lots of people were saying we were the posh version of TOWIE

Of course, plenty of people hated it. I guess it was a bit like Marmite. Loads of critics and viewers criticised us for being posh and ridiculous, and some really nasty stuff was said on Twitter. It annoyed me that some people thought we were all the same. I've always worked for my money and I'm not stuck-up. I felt like I was different from some of the others. Ollie, Cheska, Gabriella and I didn't take ourselves too seriously. Later I wrote about it for the *Huffington Post*, arguing that the view of us as 'gilded socialites', 'spray-tanned exhibitionists' and 'privately educated, hedonistic' youngsters is lazy, narrow-minded and backwards-looking. I'm not rich or shallow and have always worked hard.

Like most shows, the audience slowly increased – to 700,000 some nights – and people started to warm to it and get hooked. In the same way that *TOWIE* had become my guilty pleasure, the show became other people's regular Monday-night viewing. I loved getting Tweets from people and, if I wasn't completely hectic, would always try to respond to them, thanking them for their comments, or asking them what they thought about the show.

We toasted the series at the end of June at the club Tuatura on the King's Road. After watching the season finale, where we all went to the polo for the day and obviously more drama ensued, we gathered on the rooftop of the bar and had some drinks in the sunshine. Hilariously, before the party, Cheska and I were busted lining our stomachs in McDonald's and we smiled and joked with the photographers as we put in our orders. I quickly realised that I couldn't go and have a cheeky fast-food dash like I used too before, without being caught out. I also soon learned that I have to be careful when I do go out, because I can't be drunk and get away with it like I used to before I started starring in the show. It would be picked up by the press, or people would Tweet me the next day, telling me they had seen me pissed and dancing like a crazy woman – or even worse, had taken a picture of me!

As the season drew to a close, the team announced that there would be a second series. It goes without saying that we were all over the moon.

My top etiquette essentials

Even though I don't consider myself one of the posh Chelsea gang, I know I've had a good grounding and have learned a few manners along the way. Here are my tips on getting by without offending anyone.

Meet and greet
When meeting someone, pretend to be really excited – even if it is your ex or your ex's new girlfriend and they are the last person on earth you want to see. Lean in and give them two kisses on the cheek – the right followed by the left – and do make contact with the cheek. The air-kissing thing just makes people look a bit stupid, in my opinion. Always compliment the females and thank the guys when they say something nice to you.

Table manners
Food-fighting aside, it's always good to follow a few rules when you're at the table. Wait until everyone is served before you dive into your food – the host will normally lead.

Cutlery crises
In terms of cutlery, it goes from the outer implements

inwards. Hold your wine glass by the stem by pinching it between your thumb and forefinger.

Dinner parties

When invited to a dinner party, always take a gift for the host. My favourite option is – yes, you've guessed it – wine or flowers. When you are a host, always accept gifts graciously, but don't feel like you have to drink the wine people have brought with them.

Don't forget a thank-you

If you've been invited to a dinner party, always follow up with a thank-you card, email or phone call. I always think this is a really important gesture to make.

Phones

When you're on a date or with friends, switch your phone to silent and never have it on the table. You can always take a sneaky peek when you're in the loo or discreetly in your bag when no one is looking.

8

BOYS, BOYS, BOYS

Before I move on to talking about life after the first series of *Made in Chelsea*, I want to tell you more about my love life and relationship history. When I was little, my first major crush was Danny Zuko from the iconic film *Grease*. I thought he was so hot and declared that I would marry him. I loved everything about him: his hair, the way he spoke, and the fact he was a T-Bird. I spent hours pretending I was Sandy and watching the film over and over again, until I knew all the words off by heart. My dad bought me a karaoke set and a small microphone and he has videos of me singing 'Summer Nights' and 'You're the One That I Want' in my best voice. I thought Sandy was so beautiful and I loved her transition from being thoroughly innocent and sweet to all vampy and sexy at the end. I adored her amazing leather combo; she just looked so cool.

One of my other favourite films was *Dirty Dancing* and I was crazy about Patrick Swayze and his beautiful muscles. I love dancing and the music from the film is brilliant. For years, I was a bit obsessed with both films and I would dance along to the soundtracks almost every day.

When I was older I moved on to fancying Jude Law after watching the films *Alfie* and *Closer*. Minty and Amanda shared my crush, so we would all curl up on the sofa and eat M&Ms and stare at Jude. We spent hours dreaming up ways we could engineer a meeting and wondered out loud how good he was in bed.

When it comes to matters of the heart, I was what they call a 'young starter'. I remember kissing my boyfriend John at nursery when I was three. I couldn't tell you what he looked like, but I remember the kissing being very wet. We used to walk to the playground and I remember hiding behind one of the sheds and him diving towards me for a kiss. Worryingly, I didn't put up much of a fight, but I do remember that he used to want to hold my hand all the time in the playground and show me off, but I was having none of it and would shrug him off.

When it comes to matters of the heart, I was what they call a 'young starter'

When I was tiny I had huge crushes on all of my brother's friends; every single one of them was gorgeous. They all had amazing skin, big hair and were really funny and friendly towards me. They used to tease me loads, but in a really affectionate way, which made me love them even more. When they came over to Endlewick House, I would hang on to their every word and used to hope that one day, when I lived in London, one of them would fall in love with me.

My first true unrequited love was for a boy at St Andrew's

called Roman. He was blond, chiselled and gorgeous, like some sort of pin-up, aged ten. He was Russian and boarded because his parents were always travelling for work, and we were always in classes together because his English wasn't great and I was in the bottom sets

My first true unrequited love was for a boy at St Andrew's called Roman

because of my learning difficulties. I hated lessons, so my main focus at school would be engineering it so I could see him or sit next to him. If he was ill or off school for any reason, in my mind it would be a proper disaster and I would be bitterly disappointed. He was very naughty, but had a glint in his eye and a charm about him and he was the most popular boy in our year; even the teachers loved him. He also had this great smell and I would know if he had walked down the corridor before me. He was obviously wearing aftershave at quite a young age because he smelt really good. I realised then how important it is for boys to smell nice.

For one week, during the time of my crush, with Roman barely noticing me, I moved my affections on to a guy called James and even wrote in my notepad, 'I love JC.' When I came back into the classroom one day, I found that not only had James discovered my notepad, but he had shown my scribble to all his friends, which was absolutely mortifying. However, it was Roman whom I really adored, but I knew I never really stood a chance because he had this gorgeous girlfriend called Hannah, who was blonde and slim and really popular, just like him. I remember we used to sit in the library and they would be on the sofa snogging and I thought it was so unfair that I wasn't one of the cool girls.

I had my first kiss with a boy called Ed. He was half Brazilian and was also in my year at St Andrew's. I was about eleven and we used to hang out loads, until everyone said we were boyfriend and girlfriend. We had our first snog in the library, on one of the beanbags, during free time one evening. The kiss was nothing to write home about: it was like a washing machine in my mouth and he tasted a bit strange. I remember it feeling so weird that, as soon as the big event was over, I made some ridiculous excuse and rushed back to the boarding house and brushed my teeth and tongue profusely for about five minutes, to try to get the strange taste out of my mouth. My friends found me there and were shouting, 'You kissed Ed! Oh my God, that's so weird, urrrgggghhhhh,' like girls do, and I felt even more grossed out. Immediately afterwards, I decided I had had enough of boys and moved on to ponies. They were far more interesting.

I decided I had had enough of boys and moved on to ponies. They were far more interesting

It was a good few years before I even considered dating a boy properly. There was a brief interlude with the washer-upper at the pub. Flirting with him seemed like fun. He was a bit older and had his own car, which seemed pretty cool in my mind at the time. I was thirteen and was experimenting with make-up. I wasn't too bothered about it, but it was fun trying all the different colours and styles. Mum had given me this big pink palette for Christmas, with loads of eye shadows, lipsticks and mascaras, and I would always show up at the pub sporting some awful sparkly green or blue eye shadow, thinking I looked good. I wasn't the most attractive teen, it must be said. By the time he did eventually try to kiss me, I had learned that he had a girlfriend and I was appalled, so that was that.

Back at St Bede's, after my time living at Ba Ba's flat in Brighton, I got back into fancying boys. By then, Letty and I were as thick as thieves and we used to fancy some of the older boys and giggle as they came past in the corridors and say 'Fiiiiiit' under our breath, sometimes too loudly so they'd hear us. Then we would burst into fits of laughter and run off, trying to pull each other's kilts off. We also took a real fancy to the 'gappies' – the guys who came to help out during their gap years. We used to give them all names, like 'brown jumper guy' and 'mystery blue eyes'.

The St Bede's uniform was a white shirt, black jumper and black and white tartan kilts and one of our favourite tricks was pulling each other's kilts off. Mum always wanted my skirt to be the regulation below-the-knee length and refused to let me have it any higher, so I used to roll it up loads of times, so I had a big wedge under my jumper, and I couldn't fasten it up. I was such an easy target and would often find myself running around with no skirt on. The boys at St Bede's were quite naughty, just like Letty and me. Sometimes they would try to rip our skirts off and drag us down to the pond in the grounds of the school and pretend they were going to drown us, but Letty and I were pretty strong, so always managed to escape.

On one occasion while we were at St Bede's, Letty and I were messing around one weekend on her farm. She was doing photography as one of her options, so we thought it would be funny to take our clothes off and do some tasteful shots covering our bits with silk scarves, leaning up against trees. We used an SLR camera with a black and white film and pranced around a bit, snapping away, thinking that it would be really amusing when we developed them. We planned to hide them away never to be seen again. The film was in Letty's camera and, without thinking about it, she took it into school one day, because she had a photography lesson, and somehow we let it slip to some friends that we'd taken these funny photos over the weekend. To cut a long story short, two of the girls managed to get into Letty's locker during their break and stole the film. They developed it in the school's darkroom and photocopied about thirty or forty massive versions of some of the pictures and then handed them out to people around the school, pinned them up on noticeboards and basically distributed them all over the place, for maximum embarrassment.

The first thing we knew about it was when we were sitting in the boarding house and someone came and told us that there were semi-naked pictures of us everywhere. Initially, we were like, 'Yeah, funny,' thinking it was a joke. When they insisted, we checked Letty's camera and saw that the film had been taken. It was so awful; we started freaking out. To make matters worse, in the distance, we could hear people screaming and laughing and saw the boys running round with these pieces of paper. We were hiding and laughing ourselves, but we had no idea what to do. We literally locked ourselves away for hours, but we knew we had to get back to our classes and face the rest of the school eventually.

When we emerged, we could see that some of the pictures had been put in the pond in the school's grounds and they were floating about, facing upwards, and we couldn't get to them. The boys were all bundling on top of each other to try to get the remaining copies. It was so embarrassing. Of course, it soon blew over, but for months everyone thought it was really funny, calling us legends, and for a long time we would find the odd picture around the place, pinned on a board or in the corners of various classrooms.

There was one guy at school that I fancied loads, called Ben. He had massive Afro hair and a beautiful face, but when I did finally get together with him, it was a huge disappointment

When it actually came to the reality of dating, I wasn't so keen

because he was a terrible kisser. We would snog every night by the bus stop before we went home. I was about fourteen then and I used to love the idea of having a boyfriend, but when it actually came to the reality of dating, I wasn't so keen. I didn't want to have sex and I didn't want boys coming to Lilac Cottage, so my romance with Ben finished pretty promptly.

Before I joined St Bede's, a guy called Jimmy was there and he used to date this really popular girl a couple of years above us. Jimmy was a really talented guitarist and left St Bede's to go to music school in London. After he left and I joined, we some-how connected online and started talking. It was before the days of Facebook, so we would speak on MSN Messenger and on the webcam every night after school. I used to write little notes in my diary, stupid questions and little things I had done in the day, to prompt myself with in case the conversation dried up. I remember being so excited and so nervous at the same time when we spoke. Sometimes he would play the guitar down the phone or over the webcam and I would just melt inside. In my eyes, he was like a proper rock star. It was complicated – as much as these things can be complicated when you're fifteen – by the fact that I was terrified that the girl who used to date him would find out and hate me. Every time I saw her with her group of friends during lunchtimes and free periods at school, I was convinced she had found out and was giving me evil stares and planning how to make my life hell.

Eventually, after we had been speaking online for a few weeks, Mum drove me up to London to see him at his flat there. I was always really open with her about boys and Mum spoke to his parents beforehand to tell them I was going. He lived in a huge new apartment in Chelsea. When he greeted me at the door, it was a bit awkward because we hadn't actually met in the flesh before. My first impressions were that he had this huge rock-star hair and that he smelt amazing. He sat and played the guitar to me for ages, which was actually a bit boring, and we had a bit of a kiss on the sofa, but nothing more than that. Mum then called and said she was going for dinner with AL in town and asked me if I wanted to come along with Jimmy. He agreed and we all went for a meal together. Mum insisted on taking photos of us, which was a bit awkward. The whole family found it really funny and AL teased me mercilessly. When it was time to leave and we said goodbye with a bit of a kiss, the whole family chorused, 'Oooooh!' which was mortifying.

A few weeks later Jimmy came down to Sussex for the weekend to see me and Mum put him in a spare bedroom. Weirdly, I felt that having someone in the house was an invasion of my personal space and it made me feel a bit sick. I made Mum stay with me the entire time, so I didn't have to be alone with him.

In the end, on the Sunday, Mum and I went to do the horses and Andrew drove him to the station without us, so he could catch a train back to London. Each time I got close to a guy, I seemed to freak out a bit, especially when they came back to Lilac Cottage, and after that visit I let the relationship fizzle out.

On Saturday nights Letty and I would go into Eastbourne with our fake IDs, which were basically pieces of cardboard with Sellotape over the top. One night I met a guy called Pat, who went to one of the local schools, Eastbourne College. Pat had big blond hair and a lovely wide mouth – and we would always hang out with him and his friends, who were a bit older than us. He always smelt of Wrigley's chewing gum and the smell still reminds me of him. Sometimes I would meet him in a coffee shop in Eastbourne after school and we would talk about our days and what we had been doing. In the summer we would walk on the beach or go to the cinema. Mum always told me I had to be home by 10 p.m. and Pat was the perfect boyfriend, making sure I got back on time.

Letty and I talked about sex constantly at school and would ask everyone about the ins and outs, literally, of what was what, everything from kissing to different sexual positions, but Pat never put pressure on me to lose my virginity to him. The relationship only lasted about six months because, again, I freaked out and went off him when he got too keen.

Letty and I talked about sex constantly

When I was boarding at Taunton, during the sixth form, I met the first person whom I thought I could properly fall in love with. Tom was the older brother of a guy in my year called

George. Tom had left the year I'd arrived, after his A-Levels, so he was eighteen when I was sixteen. He had gone off to work for his dad's clothing company and was so cool. He wasn't the most gorgeous boy to look at, but everyone loved him. He was funny, sweet and charming and had the most amazing personality. He was also quite sporty and was a big skier. I was still fairly new at Taunton when I went on a night out and we met. We swapped numbers and started texting each other quite regularly. I remember I had different ringtones on my mobile phone and I used to love it when my phone buzzed and I saw his name on a little envelope on my screen. I got so excited, my palms would be all sweaty and my heart would start hammering. I couldn't open the text message fast enough to see what he had written.

He used to come and pick me up in his car after school, which was a bit naughty because it was against the school rules. We'd have a few ciders at the local pub and then he would drop me back at the boarding house, kissing me good-bye. He made me feel really, really special by telling me he was falling for me and that I was beautiful; and he was a great kisser. Sometimes I would go and stay at his parents' house at the weekend and they let us sleep in the same bed, which was a first for me. I remember painstakingly putting on my make-up and lying completely still, with my arms clamped by my side, so my make-up wouldn't run off onto the white pillows. I lay awake all night, pulling my stomach in, in case his hand touched me. I remember being really worried that I was breathing too loudly and was disturbing him. If I needed the loo in the middle of the night, it would take me about half an hour to shuffle off the bed, so I didn't wake him up. I was scared about bumping into his parents in the corridor as well. All in all, the next day, I was always pretty tired.

When we were together, one New Year's Eve, the plan was for him to come and stay with me at Lilac Cottage. I thought it might finally be time I lost my virginity. I felt ready at seventeen, so I planned it and even spoke to Mum about it, and she helped me to make my room look really nice. At the last minute, with everything arranged, Tom let me down and told me he couldn't come and see me because of a problem with his car or something like that. I was really disappointed and, later, I told him what I had been planning and he was kicking himself!

Soon after, Tom went on a skiing course for four months to a resort in France. Prior to him going away, we went round Taunton town centre picking up all the things he needed for his time away. I sneaked a look at his shopping list when he wasn't looking and one of the things on his list was condoms. I was upset and thought, 'What an idiot,' but I just blocked it out and told him I didn't want to know what he planned to do while he was away. I really missed him and used to tick off the days in my diary, counting down until he was back. It was pretty hard to keep in touch. I wasn't on Facebook then, so I would text and use MSN Messenger when I was allowed during prep hours at school, but we didn't speak much.

When the time came for his return, I went out to a bar in Taunton to wait for him and felt sick with excitement. My stomach was doing somersaults. He seemed really happy to see me and we picked up where we'd left off. We stayed together for a few more weeks, but when he decided he wanted to be a professional skier and decided to go away for a whole season, which is about five months, we made the decision to finish it. I felt like I was heartbroken and every film I watched had a starring character called Tom but, looking back, it wasn't that bad. He was a really cool guy and made my time in Somerset really fun.

When I moved to London, I was with some work colleagues at Crazy Larry's and we spotted this guy, Benjy. I remember telling one of my friends that I thought he was quite hot – he was half Filipino and a little bit older than me – and they beckoned him over, which was really, really embarrassing. We started chatting and I gave him my number. The next day he called me and invited me out to Mao Tai, a restaurant and cocktail bar on the New King's Road. It was then that I realised that I can't drink cocktails. I remember drinking the first two, but everything after that is cloudy; I was completely legless. It was that night that I lost my virginity, in Mum's bed – and, to be honest, it was a bit of a blur. By that point, I was almost nineteen and I knew I just needed to get it over with because when I met someone I really, really liked, I didn't want to still be a virgin. I felt like a bit of an idiot, to be honest.

I wanted to stay with Benjy for as long as I could after that, even though I knew it was never going to be a long-term thing. He was a really safe guy and treated me really well. He bought me a pretty necklace for Christmas and over the New Year that we were together we went to the Isle of Wight, which was lovely. But it got boring very quickly. He'd come over to my house a lot and we would watch films and, after a few weeks, we were like an old married couple. He treated me like gold, but the initial spark quickly faded, on my side at least. He wasn't working at the time, and was looking for a City job, so he was really into me and wanted to see me all the time when I wasn't at work.

After a few months, I remember thinking, 'I can't do this much longer.' One day he picked me up from work in his car. I had phoned him that day and told him I needed to speak to him about something important, so I think he knew I was going to dump him. He had given up smoking a few months beforehand, but as I got into his car, I saw that he had about forty Marlboro Lights stacked up on the dashboard, in preparation for 'the conversation'. I reckon dumping someone is sometimes far worse than being dumped. I felt awful about hurting him, but I was happy to be single again.

I reckon dumping someone is sometimes far worse than being dumped

After my break-up with Benjy, I snogged a couple of my brother's friends – the day had finally arrived after years of waiting! Understandably, my brother was less impressed with the situation, but it was just a bit of fun.

The next man in my life was Simon, who worked on the door at Embargo, a club on the King's Road. One day at work I added him on Facebook and although he claims to have waited ages before accepting me, I'm sure it was pretty instant! In the end, he got my number off a mutual friend and we met up. He was a big thinker and was really emotional and we would have long, meaningful chats. He was also really into his music, like me, and we would swap albums and go to gigs together. He was really romantic and a proper gentleman. One night he surprised me with tickets for a James Vincent McMorrow concert and he didn't tell me until we got there. On another occasion,

I got so drunk at Embargo that I passed out in one of the loos. One of my friends took me outside and I managed to hail a cab, which took me to this random address on Chelsea Embankment. I don't know why, but I think perhaps I thought there was an after-party. I managed to get through this building's huge glass doors, but couldn't get out again. I was basically locked in and was really drunk. It was three in the morning and I called Simon and all I could tell him was that I could see water and blue lights. I don't know how he did it, but he eventually found me, rescued me and took me home.

The relationship eventually ended because I think he thought I was a bit crazy. I was going out all the time then and I don't think he could deal with my partying. When we broke up, I was gutted about it for a long time. He knew he could get me back whenever he wanted, so we were on and off for a while, but in the end, I managed to say no and that was it. Not in a million years was it going to work. After all the stuff that happened during the first series of the show, when he came out to see me in Chamonix, we're still good friends and see each other around in Chelsea and on nights out.

I briefly dated a guy called Toby, who was working as an estate agent. Mum says he looked like Shaggy from *Scooby-Doo*. He had a goatee beard and took great delight in being really scruffy. His jeans had massive holes in them. He was never keen on me taking part in the show; like some of my family, he just thought it was a bad idea. The romance was fairly short-lived and it was very soon after I finished with him that I met Charlie. After saying I would never fall in love, the unthinkable happened and I fell head over heels for him.

How to get the perfect look for a date

Getting ready for a first date – especially one with a Chelsea boy – is always really nerve-wracking. Naturally you want to look and feel gorgeous. I never spend too long agonising over what to wear and keep things simple when it comes to my make-up, because I think most guys prefer the natural look, rather than a heavily made-up face. Here are my tried and tested ideas:

Clothes

👑 When it comes to clothes for an evening date, wear something classy and elegant, but sexy at the same time, like a tight pair of leather trousers and a nice top which shows off a bit of flesh. Or opt for a pair of teeny-tiny shorts and a long-sleeved top.

👑 For a daytime affair, like going to the park or bowling, choose something more low-key, like skinny jeans and a cute tee that shows off your figure in subtle way.

👑 The secret weapon, in my opinion, is a pair of high heels, because they will elongate your legs and make you feel great.

👑 I think you can really dress up a plain and simple high-street outfit with designer accessories, like

➡

a colourful clutch or an interesting chunky statement necklace.

Hair

👑 In Chelsea, everyone has big hair. A good first-date style is the half-up, half-down look. I start styling mine by using a root-boost spray, like Tigi Catwalk Session Series. Spray it through dry hair, starting at the roots, then make a side parting and clip the central section away from your face.

👑 Take sections of your hair and wrap them around your straighteners and release, so you have waves of soft curls. Make sure you twist them all in the same direction. After you have done all your hair, loosen the curls to make them look natural and use a powder, like Big Sexy Hair Powder Play, to add body.

👑 Take sections of your hair at the crown and backcomb two inches from the roots using a comb, then comb your hair through to give a smooth finish. Tie some of your hair up with a tie and secure it with a kirby grip. Finally add a good spritz of hairspray to keep the look in place.

Make-up

👑 Before putting my make-up on, I prep my face with

a skin perfector, like Clarins' Instant Light Complexion Perfector, a dewy highlighter, which I blend into the highest part of my cheekbones, the bridge of my nose, forehead and upper lip line. From there, I apply a lightweight foundation and a small amount of concealer to disguise dark circles under my eyes.

 I love the smoky-eye look and use a palette like Clarins' Eye Quartet Mineral Palette in Rosewood. The colours are browns and nudes, so you get a natural finish. Start by blending the lightest colour across your lids, which will act as a base. Then take the angled brush and apply the darkest colour along the lash line and smudge it out at the corner. Then use the pinky-brown shadow at the outer edge of the eyelid, to smooth the colour in. Apply the darker shade under the eye to add definition. Then add mascara to both your upper and lower lashes. I like bareMinerals' Flawless Definition Mascara.

As anyone who watches *Made in Chelsea* will know, from the very first episode, where I even gave Ollie Locke an extra going-over, I've always got my Rimmel Sunshimmer bronzer with me. Blend it under the cheekbones with a large brush for a sculpted, sun-kissed look.

♛ Kissable lips are very important, so give your pout a hint of colour with a product like Stila's Convertible Colour for Lips and Cheeks in Fuchsia. Add a dab of Vaseline and, voilà, you're ready to go!

Tips on dating a Chelsea boy

If there is a Chelsea boy on your radar – there have been plenty on mine over the years – follow my tips to make sure you snare him before another girl does.

♛ If you're out and see a guy you like, smile and wait for him to come over. Be cool, funny and collected and don't take yourself too seriously. And don't get really drunk and embarrass yourself. I am still learning this one!

♛ Don't tell him everything about yourself immediately; always keep a little bit back, to keep him intrigued. I think guys love elusive and mysterious women. And no matter how tempting, don't discuss ex-partners and lovers.

♛ Don't let them pay for everything, otherwise they will think pretty quickly that you are with them for their money. I always offer to pay on a date, no matter what, but if a boy lets you pay for more than half, he's a no-go, but in my opinion, it's the right thing to offer to go Dutch.

👑 It's important to get on the good side of his friends, so make sure you always make an effort to chat to them when you're all out together. Ask them questions about themselves and laugh at their jokes.

👑 Invite your man over to your house from time to time, rather than always going to his place. Light some scented candles and, if you have a fireplace, light a fire for a really romantic atmosphere.

👑 My mum always says the way to a boy's heart is through his stomach, so find out what his favourite meal is and learn to cook it.

👑 Make sure you have your own interests away from him and your life doesn't morph into his. Also, I don't think that being available all the time is attractive to a guy, so occasionally make sure you are busy – or at least say you are busy – when he wants to see you. I hate playing games, but this tactic does often work.

👑 Never, ever bombard a boy with messages and calls. Always wait for him to call you first. And if you do call and he doesn't pick up, don't call him a hundred more times to try to find out where he is. He might think you are a bit crazy!

9

HIGH, LOWS AND A
BROKEN HEART

It was the spring of 2011 and one of those nights when I really
didn't want to go out, but there was an event on at the Bluebird
and all my friends were going so I decided to drag myself off the
sofa and go along. I was with my friend Lulu at the bar when I
saw these two guys. Lulu introduced us; their names were Ollie
and Charlie. Lulu told me Charlie was one of the owners of the
restaurant and club 86, on the Fulham Road. *Made in Chelsea*
used to film there quite a lot. It is a really decadent venue, with
a restaurant and bar on the ground floor and another galleried
area on the first floor, where they serve drinks and have live
music and DJs. Charlie has great eyes and an incredible smile
and I don't know what it was about him, but I immediately felt
drawn to him. It feels pretty strange saying it now, but it was a
feeling I had never had before and I knew instantly that I wanted
to be with him. Charlie invited Lulu and I back to 86, so we left
the Bluebird, hopped in a black cab and went with them.

After we arrived, I immediately started on the champagne and ordered loads of Jägerbombs. I think I was showing off a bit, because I really fancied Charlie, and I think whatever I was doing was working because he was looking at me and laughing, while I downed the shots. All of us partied until the early hours and I went home hoping Charlie would get in touch. The next day he added me on Facebook and I remember analysing all his pictures, to try to find out more about him. I could see that he had spent some time out in Verbier, where he ran a club called Coco, and he just seemed cool and fun. When I got to know him better, I found out that everyone knew him as 'the last man standing'. If there was a party or someone wanted to go out after a club, they would ring Charlie and he would always say yes.

A week or so later, Gabriella, Cheska and I went to the Ship in Wandsworth. I had been thinking about Charlie a lot after the first meeting. I got so drunk, I was dancing on the tables along to the live band that was playing. Completely in my own world, as I partied away, I remember looking down and seeing Charlie looking straight up at me, smiling, and his eyes were shining. It felt just like fate. Apparently he'd told Lulu that he fancied me and she'd obviously told him that I really liked him too. I jumped down from the table and I could tell he was quite nervous as we chatted. He was really complimentary and told me I looked lovely. I really hoped that something would happen. He was heading off to another party, but before he did he put his number in my phone and told me he would be in touch. By that point, I was really wrecked, so I took matters into my own hands and called him to tell him I was on my way to Fiesta Havana, which is this club on the Fulham Broadway. I shouldn't have been allowed in, because I was wearing flip-flops, and in the end, I cut my foot really badly on some stray glass on the dance floor. Blood was pouring everywhere, but I was too drunk to really care.

Outside, my phone started ringing and Charlie told me he was at a party at his friend's house in Embankment. I decided to skip going to A&E and met him there, and we wrapped my foot up in loads of napkins. The house where this guy was hosting the party was incredible, with floor-to-ceiling glass windows looking out over the River Thames. There was a terrace with a glass floor and the views over the city were incredible. I ended up trying to flirt with another guy, to see what Charlie would do, and he took the bait. In the end, he came over and we got rid of the other guy and sat together on a beanbag on this glass floor, so it felt like we were suspended in the air. I remember him pulling me towards him and we had this long, passionate kiss, and it was just glorious. It was the best kiss of my life.

It was the best kiss of my life

Charlie lived near me, in a flat on the Wandsworth Bridge Road, and at the beginning it was the easiest relationship I have ever been in. He was very open with me, there was no game-playing and it was just fun. Very quickly, we started spending a lot of time together. Lulu and I would rock up at 86 most nights after work, and this was during the summer, so we would all sit outside and get drunk together. Lulu started going out with Charlie's business partner, Matt, so the four of us were always together. It was an amazing summer.

However, slowly, the constant drinking and partying started to take its toll and I would often wake up looking and feeling rank. I was still working at LingBridge then so I was often exhausted. The relationship with Charlie was all-consuming and I was totally in love with him, so I put him first. It was incredibly intense and I couldn't concentrate on anything else. I remember, on nights out, he sometimes mouthed over to me, 'I love you.' It was the first time anyone had told me that they loved me and I was completely blown away. It was so all-consuming that I was terrified that something would go wrong and I would mess up somehow.

At first we didn't argue, but it felt quite tumultuous at times. I was often jealous because he was always at the club, hosting nights and chatting to other girls, which was part of his job. To try to make myself feel better about it, I was always there,

I was often jealous because he was always at the club, chatting to other girls

which wasn't particularly healthy for either of us. By then I had moved out of Kate's house and was living in a flatshare nearby, but I hated it. My bedroom was in the basement and I didn't know my flatmates very well. I didn't even have proper wardrobe space, so my room was always a complete mess, with clothes and shoes strewn all over the floor. As a result, I was always at Charlie's house. He shared with a guy called Eddie, who would always look after me if I was upset about Charlie or feeling insecure. He would hug me and tell Charlie off if he had done something to upset me. I always felt far more comfortable at their house than at my own.

I knew that at some point the relationship would burn out and when I felt like it was slipping away from me, I became really clingy and insecure. I was invading Charlie's personal space so much that clearly he was getting sick of the relationship. He would sometimes lie to me and say he wasn't going out and then he would. One night, I called him to tell him I was on the way to 86 to see him, but he told me not to, insisting that he was on his way home to bed. Then I went past Kosmopol, another club on the Fulham Road, in a black cab and I saw him outside, surrounded by loads of women. He was chatting to them and laughing. I asked the cab to stop and dragged him to one side and was screaming and shouting: 'How dare you lie to me?' All he could say was that I was 'crazy'. He often called me 'psycho', which drove me mad. I think he turned me into a crazy person and that was part of the reason I stayed with him. Previously, I just used to get bored so quickly, but he kept me on my toes by being mean to me. Another thing he would call me was 'Big Whale', saying I had put on weight with all the drinking, which was probably true, but nonetheless, it's not exactly nice to hear.

In July 2012, after we had been dating for over a year, he came with me to the wedding of my stepsister Minty to her boyfriend Lorenzo in Porto Ercole in Italy. Minty had met Lorenzo, who was working at Credit Suisse at the time, at a nightclub. By then, Amanda was dating her boyfriend – and now husband – a chartered surveyor called Brook, and the four of them are very close and big party animals and sometimes we would go out with them. The wedding was fantastic and Minty looked incredible, but I remember getting so drunk the night before we were due to go home that Charlie and I had a huge argument. As everyone got together to drive to the airport, I just couldn't stop crying. In the end, I stayed in Italy and spent a few days in Rome and did a bit of sightseeing, trying to sort my head out and work out what I wanted.

When we argued, I would often go round to Lorenzo and Minty's house and they would look after me. I knew Charlie was no good for me and everyone told me all the time that I had to finish it. One morning, to gauge his reaction, I said to him, 'We have to finish this.' When he agreed, I was so angry with myself for saying it and was distraught. Inevitably, we got back together a few weeks later, but by then, the damage had been done. I was even more insecure than before and I just wanted to go out the whole time to try to block it out.

We kept breaking up and getting back together again, but in the end, he had to dump me, because I couldn't finish it myself. I'd told Mum that it was over, but I think she knew it wasn't. One night she secretly stayed in my flat, because she knew I had work the next day. As she'd predicted, Charlie was such a bad influence on me, and we rolled in at 5 a.m. and I had to be up at 7.30 a.m. Mum woke me up as late as she could, but I couldn't focus at all and I had a *I was* screaming row with Charlie. In the end, *heartbroken* when I was out of the room, Mum told him, 'If you think anything of Binky, you can get out of her life forever.' He screamed and shouted and left – and that was it. That was the end of the end.

I was heartbroken. The worst part was having to drive past 86 and the fear of bumping into him when I was out. I was distraught and hated being in the house alone, so I went out all the time. My self-esteem had hit rock bottom.

I wasn't in a good way. Sometimes after big night outs, I would have panic attacks. It felt like I couldn't breathe and my heart was hammering really fast. I couldn't stop crying and couldn't concentrate on anything. I felt so depressed and like I was the only one who had ever felt that bad. Some nights I couldn't sleep after going out and often, in the morning, I just felt like I couldn't get out of bed. At times, I didn't feel like I would ever recover. It's almost like I had forgotten how to be the person I was before I met Charlie.

On one particularly bad day, I was at Ollie Locke's flat and Cheska was there with us. In the end, Cheska rung my mum and explained that they were really worried about me. I was just lying on the sofa, crying my eyes out, saying that I hated my life. I was a complete mess. Mum immediately drove up from Sussex to the flat and bundled me into the car and we drove home. After a few days of more tears and talking, I started eating healthy food again, sleeping properly for the first time in ages and doing some proper exercise. I needed a complete break, because I couldn't think straight, let alone function normally.

A major way I knew I could make my life better was by moving out of my horrible flat into somewhere more comfortable, sharing with people I liked. One day, during the time I spent at home, Letty and another friend, Lucy, were visiting and we decided to look for a house together in Fulham. We had talked about it for years and with Letty finally finishing her university degree, it was the right time for her to move to London too. That was the beginning of me picking myself back up again. I thought back to the times when I was a teenager and the 'bull in a china shop' analogy and, after a few days, everything didn't seem quite so awful.

So I started to have a healthier lifestyle, and Letty, Lucy and I began hunting for a new house in Parsons Green. We spent the day going around looking at places, but no one really took us seriously, because we were quite young, so in the end, we went with my mum and Letty's mum. There was one estate agent who showed us around who was so nervous he fumbled with the keys as he let us into each of the houses, and we took the mickey out of him mercilessly. We are still friends now and I often pop in and say hi when I go past his office. After another couple of days of house-hunting, we found the perfect place, with a big living area, kitchen and garden and bedrooms for all of us. It was September 2012 when we moved in our stuff and, very quickly, it was back to the good old days, behaving like we were teenagers again, being particularly juvenile. In the first week, we popped into Tesco for some supplies and I loaded Letty up with lots of bottles of Coke. When her arms were completely rammed, I pulled down her trousers and she couldn't do anything but sink to the floor in hysterical laughter.

I sometimes joke that 'to get over someone, you need to get under someone'

I sometimes joke that 'to get over someone, you need to get under someone' and I started to feel better again when I began dating a guy called Henry. He is an old family friend and had been in and out of my life since school. His family are farmers and he's like a big, soft Labrador. It started when I was in a local pub called the Cricketers with Mum and, out of the blue, Henry texted me, asking how I was and if I fancied a drink. Together, Mum and I dreamt up a suitable response and, after telling me my chat was great (thanks, Mummy Felstead!) and speaking on Facebook for a while, we started dating properly. I loved the idea of dating a farmer and could picture myself back in the country, chained to an Aga, with three kids, loads of horses and dogs. He'd be the perfect husband and, for a while, I thought I could marry him. He was calm and wasn't a big party animal. I used to get the train down to see him and we would go for long walks and pub lunches, and he would come up to London to visit me. I was in Sussex a lot more and it was very comforting and homely. It did me a lot of good at the time because I was so fragile.

In the end, the distance became an issue. Sometimes he was a bit stuffy and would say things that upset me. I hate confrontation, but I made it clear I wasn't happy, so things ended. However, slowly but surely, I had started to feel a bit better about Charlie, and my brief relationship with Henry was a big part of my recovery.

Looking back at my romance with Charlie, I think it was a case of it being a very big relationship when I was too young for it. I know everyone has their first loves, but this was a particularly damaging one. I have heard from mutual friends that he is living on the Isle of Wight and he has come to realise that he has lost me as a friend. I will always care for him, but I know that I am much happier without him in my life.

I know that I am much happier without him in my life

Top tips to heal a broken heart

There's no question about it: splitting up with someone is one of the worst feelings in the world, especially if it wasn't your decision. Here are a few things I have found have helped me in the past:

♕ Seek support from your family and friends. These are the people in your life who know you best and can support you when the chips are down. If you have a good relationship with your parents, great, but if not, use the break-up as a chance to reconnect with them and seek their support.

♕ Don't call or message your ex. Chances are, this will only result in an on-off, on-off break-up, which just prolongs the agony. Try to get on with your life and think, 'What is meant to be is meant to be.' Remember, things happen for a reason and there is someone lovely just around the corner waiting for you. That guy just wasn't the one and he has to go so this other guy can come into your life.

♕ Get active. Putting on your trainers and going for a run or heading to the gym may feel like the last thing you want to do, but exercise will trigger feel-good endorphins, which will help to lift your spirits.

➡

I find that running outside in the fresh air really helps me to clear my head and gives me a chance to think.

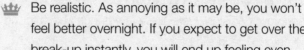 Be realistic. As annoying as it may be, you won't feel better overnight. If you expect to get over the break-up instantly, you will end up feeling even worse. Give yourself some time to feel better. It's such a huge cliché, but time is the best healer of all.

Avoid unhealthy behaviours, even though you may want to go out every night to make yourself feel better. This may help in the short term, but the next day you will feel even worse because alcohol is a depressant. Also, drinking excessively is damaging to your health.

Change your habits. If a certain album or singer reminds you of an ex, switch them off for the time being. If you lived together, remove your ex's belongings from your bedroom and the rest of your home. Move the furniture around to make it feel different and new.

Delete their number from your phone. This will stop you sending drunken text messages, telling them that you miss them, or being tempted to call during a weak moment.

👑 Eat well. You may have lost your appetite – or want to pig out on junk food – but this will leave you feeling more miserable and drained than before. Try to eat healthy, nutritious meals. There's not much a good Sunday roast can't cure.

👑 Make sure you're happy with your home. Your home is just that, so make sure you are content with where you are living and, if you are sharing with other people, it is really important that you like and get on with your flatmates.

👑 Know when to seek professional help. There is a fine line between the two, but sometimes heartbreak can spill over into depression and anxiety. See a counsellor if you can.

10

MORE SW3 DRAMAS

By the start of the second series, Ollie had started dating Chloe Green, who is the daughter of Sir Philip Green, who, among other business ventures, owns one of my favourite shops, Topshop. I didn't know her and, at the start, didn't want to like her because I had Gabriella to look after and I am very protective of Ollie. However, the four of us – Ollie, Cheska, Chloe and I – went on a weekend fishing break, so we could get to know her better, and we got on brilliantly. She was really normal and fun. She also got me thinking more about fashion. We went round Topshop together and she got all her favourite personal shoppers working on me and made loads of suggestions about the clothes that she thought would look good on me. It was a bit like *Pretty Woman* – we would walk out of the shops with loads and loads of bags. She also got me into doing my nails more than twice a year, because I always admired hers, so I started having them done professionally with her.

In terms of my friendships, it was still very much a case of Ollie, Cheska and me keeping ourselves to ourselves, but slowly, during that series, I started to hang out with the likes of Spencer, Rosie and Louise. I really liked them all and there was no one whom I didn't get on with.

During the filming of series two, Gabriella was going through a really crazy time and she wrote a song for Ollie called 'Fight' and cast an Ollie look-a-like for her music video. This seemed a bit weird to me. I told her that it was a bad decision, but she wouldn't listen to me. It had got to the point where I didn't know what else I could say to stop her from being so upset about her break-up with Ollie, and she constantly asked me about him. I tried to tell her that it was time to move on, but I know she was finding it very hard and was stuck in a bit of a rut.

My relationship with Cheska became quite difficult

It was also around that time that my relationship with Cheska started to become quite difficult. At this point I was still spending a lot of time with Charlie and had met a new bunch of friends through him, so we were spending less time together. We are both Geminis, so are really stubborn, always think that we're right and refuse to back down. She was always telling me off for getting drunk with Charlie and I was getting annoyed with her for treating me like a child. I also became very friendly with Lulu and I don't think Lulu and Cheska got on that well, so that didn't help matters. I don't think we communicated very well about how we felt about the distance between us, so we continued to grow apart. Also,

I felt a bit like Cheska had taken Ollie away from me, because they moved in together, and that was a large part of why I was upset.

Spencer and I had always got on and I became his 'sexy agony aunt' figure. I was seeing more of other friends and I think Cheska was upset that I wasn't seeing her as much. I love Spenny. I know he's really naughty, but I always say, when people ask me about him, that he's doing what plenty of guys his age do and, on a more personal note, he's never treated me badly. Whenever we are out together, we sit on our own for hours, talking about our family, life and relationships. Of course, I tell him he's an idiot when he messes up

Spencer and I had always got on and I became his 'sexy agony aunt' figure

and cheats on his girlfriends. However, I do respect the fact that he is totally honest and true to himself, like I am, and I don't think he particularly cares about how he comes across. When people question him, he says, 'I like girls, that's just me,' and I respect his honesty. When he said in his book that he's slept with 1000 women, I thought that could be just showing off, because that is a lot of girls! I mean, is he counting? Surely once you get into those kinds of figures, you lose track? I'll always be there for him if something happens, but you can't really tell him what to do. All I say to him is, 'Make sure you always pick up the phone when I call and don't change.'

The time when I bumped into Cheska in the supermarket and I told her Spencer had invited me to Morocco with the others, I could tell she was really put out, but as I drifted away from her and Ollie, I had to make other friends. I did miss her, but wasn't confrontational about what had been going on. Watching the show back, I felt quite awkward about what had happened, but we didn't really talk about it. I think she felt like she was the victim in all of it, saying that the ball was in my court.

At that time, things were going downhill with Charlie too, so it was good to be invited away. In Morocco, I hung out with Caggie and Millie a lot. They are great girls and really good fun, and we chatted quite openly about their relationships and our lives. The group were quickly learning that I sometimes came out with some pretty stupid comments and Jamie was always taking the piss out of me. Memorably, he asked me what the capital of Africa is – and it clearly isn't South Africa!

I kept working at LingBridge for as long as I possibly could, but in the end I just couldn't manage to juggle everything that was going on in my life. I was sad to say goodbye, but I knew it was the right thing to do – for them and me.

I think it's safe to say that one of the people that I didn't see eye to eye with was Kimberley Garner. I'm a very good judge of character and I could see straight through her. I was convinced she wasn't genuine. Richard Dinan is an old friend of Ollie's and I dated him years ago. We hooked up for few weeks, but it was nothing serious, even though I wanted it to be. He had this big house in the country and we used to go on walks together and it was all very sophisticated and mature. We would sometimes go clubbing or out to incredible restaurants. Ollie had warned me that Richard didn't want a serious girl-friend, but of course I didn't listen at the time and really liked him. In the show, it played out that both Cheska and Gabriella fancied him, which I thought was a bit silly, considering I had warned them what he was like. I didn't want to get involved.

Kimberley's boyfriend, Diego, was a good friend of Minty and Lorenzo's and I used to do a bit of work for him as his promoter. He was in bits about the fact she appeared to be dating Richard behind his back. Although she claims that she wasn't with Diego at the time, I thought we had to do something about it. That's just how I am; I thought he was being treated badly and I didn't want it to continue. The whole situation was blown massively out of proportion, and Richard was annoyed that we had got involved, although I do think it was aimed more at Cheska than at me, but my intention was always really genuine. Cheska and I became closer through that experience and I realised how much I had missed her.

I found Jamie funny and we became good friends. He was always game for fun and constantly flirted with me, saying he wished that I was single. He was always very jokey about it, so I didn't think too much of it at the time. When I split up with Charlie, he would say stuff like, 'Are you REALLY single? Are you sure?' He made me laugh. He knows what to say and when to say it. I was so heartbroken after the split that I was really flattered by his constant attention and when he complimented me, I felt like it was a whole new chapter of my life and time on the show. I wanted to get over Charlie and I thought I should take the plunge by going on a date with Jamie when he asked.

I was a bit nervous, but he took me on a golf date and it was really fun. Obviously I beat him hands down! The best part was driving the golf buggy; I went pretty fast in that bad boy and almost chucked Jamie out at one point. I knew there were two new boys joining the show, but I was surprised when Andy Jordan and Sam Cussins crashed the date. Jamie was very sweet and charming throughout, though, and I really started to feel like I could like him.

Jamie was very sweet and charming throughout, though, and I really started to feel like I could like him

Later, when we kissed on a night out and then at Proudlock's country house in Dorset, it felt pretty strange, as Jamie was the first person I had kissed since Charlie. The kiss wasn't too bad; he's quite a good kisser – not that good, mind ... We were coined 'Jinky' by the team, but we didn't even get to a second date, due to his indecision about what he wanted from the relationship. After telling me he could really fall for me, he was then to-ing and fro-ing for a while. When he said he 'couldn't trust' himself, I felt he had really led me on and was behaving a bit like a little boy. I was quite confused, because by that point I really liked him. It was clear he didn't really want a girlfriend. Jamie apologised profusely afterwards and admitted he had behaved badly. For a while, I think we both felt that we had lost our friendship and I think we both learnt a lesson from it. I will never put myself in that situation with somebody again.

It was nice when Mum and I spoke about Jamie, because she has so many words of wisdom, and she came out with her famous line, 'A man at twenty-three is like a girl at fifteen; they are so juvenile,' over a glass of champagne at the

Dorchester. I felt quite emotional speaking to her about it because we are so close. It was good having some support from her. Ollie was brilliant as well, having a go at Jamie on my behalf.

When Ollie, Cheska, Gabriella and I went to Amsterdam, Jamie rocked up on a tandem bike to apologise and, after that, everything seemed to blow over – but I would never go there again. However, love, or at least sex, was in the air for two of the others, and despite their sniping and bickering, I knew Ollie and Gabriella would hook up again. It came as no surprise that they had sex while we were away. They have a very good sex life, apparently, and they were both always going on about how they clicked in bed. I'm glad that it happened, because afterwards they seemed to make peace – finally! When Gabriella left for Greece, I was sad and I knew we'd miss her, but I was confident that she would be back and thought it was probably a good idea for her to go and get her head together. She was also going to work on her music out there, which was what she loved.

I had admitted that I fancied Andy Jordan and was messaging him for a while

I had admitted that I fancied Andy Jordan and was messaging him for a while. He was always telling me how much he liked me. It might seem like we had had a one-night stand, but we hadn't. I thought I could like him and was disappointed when he said he wasn't looking for anything serious. It was a case of 'another one bites the dust' – and it was yet another embarrassing occasion that I hoped my ex wouldn't see. I didn't like the fact that I was getting the 'unlucky in love' tag. I knew Andy would eventually get together with Louise, because they had both liked each other a lot for ages. I was happy for him, because I was definitely over him by that point.

Lucy Watson joined the show during series four. I didn't like her at first

Lucy Watson joined the show during series four. I didn't like her at first and didn't really want to get to know her. She was very cold and didn't go out of her way to make new friends. However, we began to hang out together and we get on really well, because we both just speak our minds and say exactly what we are thinking. I realised that when I first met her she put on a massive front because she had been hurt so badly in the past, so she comes across as really hard, but when you get to know her she's actually very sweet and caring. She is the queen of drama. She doesn't care what people think, and I love that about her.

I got really angry when people said I had dumped Cheska for Lucy. By then, Cheska had got into a serious relationship with someone she thought could be 'the one', and naturally, when a good friend starts dating someone, you see them less. She is also a few years older than me and was happy to settle down and go out less. Eventually our friendship did sort itself out, but it felt quite difficult for a while. Having said that, I've always loved Cheska. If I don't speak to her for more than a couple of days, I do miss her.

My getting-ready-to-go-out diary

Unlike lots of girls, I don't normally spend too long getting ready for a night out, but if it's a special occasion, I'll leave an hour or so to get myself together – and probably end up running a bit late!

Here is my schedule:

👑 Two weeks before – Recently I have been getting eyelash extensions, so I don't have to worry about mascara, and I love the way they make my lashes look really thick. I also get semi-permanent make-up on my eyebrows by a lady called Debra Robson, in her clinic on Harley Street (www.debrarobsonldn.co.uk). It makes my brows look more prominent than they are naturally.

👑 A week before – I have been using Easilocks extensions for a while (www.easilocks.com) and my amazing hairdresser, Mikey Kardashian, does them for me. It takes about three hours, because I have loads of extensions, and they're quite heavy, but I love them because they give me a lot more volume. Afterwards, Mikey blow-dries my hair with a big brush. I only wash it about once a week because I find that if I wash it too much, it takes the natural oils out.

A few days before – Normally I will have my tan and eyelashes done at somewhere like Glo in Fulham (www.glofulham.com) a few days before a big event. I love having my nails done and now I get them to do me with my own Binky London nail polishes (www.binkylondon.com).

 7 p.m. – I hop in the shower, shave my legs and exfoliate and moisturise all over. I'm lucky enough to have a really luxurious, feminine bathroom in my house. It's so lovely that my housemates and I are always fighting for bathroom time.

 7.30 p.m. – I will normally be going out with my friends or flatmates, so we will open a bottle of wine to drink while we are getting ready and I'll blow-dry and style my hair, making it as textured as possible. I use a curling wand and spritz loads of hairspray on it to hold it in place.

 7.45 p.m. – I do my make-up. I am a big fan of smoky eyes and nude lips and tend to always fall back on this look if I am unsure. I don't wear loads of make-up; I'm pretty low maintenance like that.

8 p.m. – It's time to decide what to wear. If it's a big event, I'll normally have an outfit in mind, so the

process isn't quite as time-consuming as it otherwise would be. I am a big fan of dresses and tight trousers and tops. I always wear heels.

 8.30 p.m. – I love accessorising and while I don't spend much money on clothes, I think designer accessories can really show off an outfit. Once I'm dressed, I'll decide on a bag and pack it with my wallet and phone, and I always carry my lip balm, MAC Face & Body Foundation and Benefit Hoola bronzer with me. I love everything from MAC. I recently had my whole make-up bag stolen and had to buy everything again. I nearly cried. It cost me an arm and a leg!

 8.45 p.m. – I always wear perfume. I am a bit of a fragrance flirt and find I fall in love with a new scent every three or four months. I love everything, from unusual niche fragrances by classic perfumers like Annick Goutal or Serge Lutens, to the blockbuster celebrity ones by the likes of J-Lo. I often fall back on old favourites like Miss Dior Cherie, which I love. I might even bring out my very own Binky perfume one day; after all, I've put in years of research!

 9 p.m. – We finish off the wine, order a black cab and are ready to go out partying.

11

SERIES FIVE AND OUR BAFTA GLORY

When I first met Phoebe-Lettice Thompson, I knew there may be fireworks because she speaks plainly and takes no prisoners. Olivia and Fran Newman-Young, and Olivia and Lucy had some sort of history to do with an ex-boyfriend, so Phoebe – and Olivia to a certain extent – were unlikely to warm to me as I was friends with Lucy.

The three girls were invited to Verbier on a skiing trip with Lucy, Andy, Jamie, Fran and me; it was a massive surprise when we realised they were there too. The way Phoebe acted towards us made it very clear we were unlikely to become firm friends at any time in the future. She's much more of a boys' girl than me and

When I first met Phoebe-Lettice Thompson, I knew there may be fireworks because she speaks plainly and takes no prisoners

most of the other girls. There was a dinner at the chalet which got really out of hand and Lucy started crying when she realised something had happened with Olivia's ex-boyfriend. It was completely pointless to dredge up stuff from the past, but we'd all had far too much to drink by that point, so I think alcohol played a big part.

One night during that trip, we went out and it all got a bit crazy. We had a table in one of the Verbier clubs and unlimited vodka to enjoy. The high altitude combined with not knowing my limits, and I got pretty blotto and gave Jamie a piece of my mind. I was a bit put out by the fact that he was so openly flirtatious with everyone else, especially Lucy and Phoebe, and I felt like I was the only girl there whom no one was talking to. We had been really friendly, but after the romance-that-never-happened, we weren't as close as we used to be.

The following day I could hardly remember a thing. When I woke up, aside from a pounding headache, I had a massive knot in my stomach about what had happened. When I asked Lucy, whom I was sharing a room with, how I had been, she said, in typical Lucy style, 'Yeah, it wasn't great.' I think I was still hurting from my break-up with Charlie and was upset. Mum stayed with me in London for a while to help me get back on track.

During that time, I was still spending less time with Ollie and Cheska, so kept myself to myself in terms of friendships. By then, Ollie had started dating Ashley James and was spending less time with his friends, which is natural. Out of all of his girlfriends, I think I got to know Ashley the least. I felt she was quite reserved, so I left them to it. In Verbier, I had got on well with Fran; she is really solid and grounded.

Afterwards, I invited her round to my house for drinks and later she moved in with me. It's great to live with someone who understands what it's like to be on the show.

One of the fun things I did during that series was a magazine shoot with Mark-Francis, where I modelled some clothes for him. He kept talking about Graff, which is an international jeweller, but I had no idea what he was talking about. In fact, half of what he says I have no clue what he means, but he is genuinely what he seems – the most outrageous man, but in a very lovely way. I think he's great, although I would never be able to sit down and have a deep and meaningful conversation with him, because he would lose me after the first sentence! Also – and maybe this is slightly inappropriate – because he has the biggest trouser bulge. Lucy and I are always staring at it!

One of the best parties I've ever been to was a barn dance that Mum and I hosted. It provided the perfect backdrop for yet more Louise/Spencer/Lucy drama, but it was quite fun and everyone made the effort to dress up in country attire. It was good to get out of the Chelsea clubs and we played hilarious country-style games, like apple bobbing and 'Splat the Rat'.

We always end every series with a show, hosted by Rick Edwards, which he dubbed 'a posh version of *Jeremy Kyle*', where we rehash everything that has happened. It's always held at the club Under the Bridge at Chelsea Football Club and we all get dolled up. Rick is great; he is very funny and there are always quite a lot of amusing sketches and games. Everyone is terrified of going on the sofa to be interviewed, because he puts us all on the spot and is just so in-your-face with his line of questioning. It is hot up there under the lights and the crowds are always booing or wolf-whistling. As long as you haven't done anything bad, you're fine.

Unsurprisingly, Spencer and Jamie never come off that well Unsurprisingly, Spencer and Jamie never come off that well. After series five, when Lucy found out that Spencer had cheated on her, it was awful, as they hadn't seen each other since. I spent a lot of time sitting with Lucy, trying to calm her down before she went on. I would never have been able to do it; she was really brave. It was very hard to watch Spencer cringing as Rick laid into him. If it were me, I would want to shout, 'Rick, shut up and stop being such a bellend!' However, the drama on the show had clearly been good for the ratings, because the opening episode of the show saw 10,000 Tweets per minute!

Growing up, I had always wanted to be on TV, so walking up the red carpet alongside some of the biggest names in the industry for a TV awards ceremony would have been my ultimate dream back when I was fifteen.

When *Made in Chelsea* first started, I don't think I ever expected it to get nominated for major TV gongs. However, the show was far more successful than any of us could've hoped for and we were first nominated for a BAFTA in 2012. The British Academy of Film and Television Arts is the biggest accolade in the industry. We were so surprised to even be nominated; it was such a massive honour and an incredible achievement. However, we all felt that we deserved it for playing our lives out in front of the cameras with the world watching. It showed just how far the show had come.

I had no idea how big the BAFTA ceremonies are; I am quite naïve about that sort of stuff. Of course, I wanted to look my best. The night before the event, I was freaking out, as I had nothing to wear and had already turned my wardrobe upside down about three times in the quest to find the perfect outfit. In the end, I got a stylist round to help me decide and she brought a load of dresses with her for me to try on. I felt quite chubby and bloated at the time and didn't like the look of anything I put on – it was complete dress-up hell. In the end, I chose a navy-blue number with detailing on the shoulders.

On the day itself, I had my hair done with Rosie beforehand, and we went with Ollie, Cheska and Gabriella to the event at the Royal Festival Hall on the South Bank.

There were loads of stars there – like Ricky Gervais, Olivia Colman, Holly Willoughby, Fearne Cotton and Miranda Hart – and I felt quite overwhelmed to be walking down the red carpet alongside them. Sadly we missed out on the award to *Young Apprentice*, but it felt like a huge achievement just to be there at all. I was still dating Charlie at this time and, after the three-course meal and the ceremony itself, I went home to him and just sat on the sofa. I didn't have a life when I was with him and never wanted to be away from him. Also, at that time, I wasn't that friendly with anyone else in the cast apart from Ollie and Cheska and didn't have the confidence to strike up conversations with people I didn't know. Sometimes I felt events like that were a bit fake and they made me quite anxious.

The 2013 BAFTA ceremony was a completely different story. We were delighted when we heard we had been nominated in the same category again, but certainly didn't expect to win. We were up against *The Audience*, *I'm a Celebrity . . . Get Me Out of Here!* and *Young Apprentice* again, and I was pretty sure *I'm a Celeb* would get it: it is such a massive show and I love it. Of course, I had another wardrobe dilemma. My outfit was an awful pink jumpsuit, which I now hate when I look back at it. I was really hungover, because I'd had a big night out with Henry, whom I was seeing at the time, the night before.

Lucy and I had our hair and make-up done by Mark Hill and MAC at a hotel nearby and then we all left together. I walked down the red carpet on my own, and it was awful weather, so my hair was all over the place, but I tried to pose as best I could and answer questions from journalists. Sometimes being on the red carpet can be quite intimidating because everyone screams your name and some of the photographers can be quite scary. I also had my picture taken with Lucy and Louise, both of whom I was quite friendly with by then and who had managed to put their animosity aside for the night and keep it civil.

> Sometimes being on the red carpet can be quite intimidating because everyone screams your name

Again the line-up was incredible and it felt amazing to be in the same room as some of the UK's biggest TV stars, like Dermot O'Leary, Sienna Miller, Damian Lewis, David Walliams and Alan Carr.

When Holly Willoughby announced us as the winners, not only was I in complete shock, but I had to make it down about a million steps without falling over, under the lights, which were roasting hot.

Once I was standing safely onstage with Spencer, Jamie, Francis, Millie, Louise, Lucy, Andy and Mark-Francis, I felt just blown away by the excitement and adrenalin. It was so surreal and I couldn't help but smile and think, 'In your face!' to all those people who had doubted my motivations back in 2010, when I first talked about the show. We all felt really honoured and couldn't wipe the smiles from our faces. I always joke now and say I want to hold the BAFTA when I walk down the aisle on my wedding day, because it is one of the things I am most proud of in my life. I was so stunned. Thank God I didn't have to speak, because I wouldn't have been able to.

Graham Norton said to the audience, 'They were insufferable before – what are they going to be like now?'

Afterwards, we headed backstage for the press conference and talked about how surprised we were at our win. We celebrated afterwards, and even though the others partied until the early hours at the Royal Festival Hall and had a big one, I headed home at a reasonable time.

After the event, the response on Twitter was really mixed. While loads of fans were celebrating with us, of course there were people who felt the need, yet again, to criticise us. Lord Sugar was clearly particularly annoyed that his show had lost out and Tweeted: '*Young Apprentice* did not win a BAFTA tonight. *Made in Chelsea* won. Can't believe it.'

I don't think we'd made any secret about the fact that we were bewildered by the whole thing. Even Ant and Dec said they would rather have lost out to *The Audience* or *Young Apprentice* rather than us, because they were 'more respectable', but I don't think we try to pretend that we are anything we are not.

Outside of the BAFTAs, there have been a couple of other awards shows, including the National Reality *Winning awards rocks!* TV Awards at Rochester Hall in August 2012 and the *TV Choice* Awards at the Dorchester in September 2013. Again, it felt like all the great and good of showbiz were there and I got so nervous. We didn't win any awards at either, but I am just excited that the show is getting so much recognition. I worry about how I will look in the pictures the next day, but I'm starting to feel more relaxed about it. Either way, winning awards rocks!

My top red-carpet posing tips

I've stood on a few red carpets since being on the show, so here are my top tips to make sure you look fab when the paparazzi take your picture:

Posture makes perfect
Always hold you head high and stand tall, with your shoulders pulled down and back. Imagine an invisible string is attached to your head, pulling you up towards the sky. Even if you're not feeling confident, this will make you appear more self-assured – and skinnier!

Thrust a hip

One of the best poses is to thrust one hip to the side and stretch out your opposite leg as far as it will go, while also pointing your toes. This will make your hips appear smaller and your legs longer.

Rotate

Another way to stand, if you're conscious of your waistline, is to rotate your upper body slightly, which will give the impression of a smaller tummy area. It's amazing what a simple twist can do!

Cross your legs

Another often-used look that I like is to cross your legs, one behind the other – it doesn't matter which goes where. This pose makes you appear thinner by narrowing your waist.

Don't pull faces

Sometimes, when I look back at pictures of myself, I think I look awful. The best photos are always the ones in which I look most relaxed and at ease, rather than like a deer caught in the headlights.

Stay focused

Some of the worst pictures are the ones taken when you are looking around and constantly fidgeting because you're feeling uncomfortable. Try to move slowly and take a few seconds to get into position before dazzling the camera with your best smile.

Don't take yourself too seriously
It might sound like an obvious point, but smile! It will make you instantly likeable. Try not to worry about what is going on around you. Just have fun!

How to get the perfect red-carpet fake tan

It must be said that I have had my fair share of fake-tan disasters. When I first discovered fake tan, when I was fifteen, I would always be showing off my very patchy legs. On some occasions, I remember having to wear gloves, because my hands were so orange from applying it with bare hands rather than using a mitt!

I always like to have a bit of colour at a big event and, most of the time, I get my tans done professionally. I also always have a spray tan done before I go on holiday – I don't want to be the whitest whale on the beach! However, from time to time, I will do them myself at home, so learn from my mistakes, girls.

Here are my top tips:

 Preparation is really important, because you need an even surface to apply the tan, so make sure you exfoliate beforehand really thoroughly. Spend more time on dry areas like wrists, knees, ankles and elbows.

Moisturise all over and let it sink in before you apply your faux glow. Again, pay particular attention to the areas that are prone to dryness.

 If you're using a lotion or a mousse, always use a mitt or glove to apply the fake tan (so you don't get bright orange hands). If you do use a glove, make sure you press your fingers together, to avoid streaks.

 I like the Rimmel Sunshimmer for a nice DIY colour. I start on my arms, then do my tummy and torso, working down to my legs.

 When it comes to the face, I use a specific facial tanner; again the Rimmel Sunshimmer is perfect for this. Apply with a foundation brush, a small mitt or a sponge, to try to ensure even coverage. A great tip is to apply Vaseline along your hairline, so you're not left with any dodgy tidemarks.

 Make sure you leave it to dry and wear dark, loose clothing for a few hours afterwards, to let the tan sink in properly without ruining any wardrobe favourites.

 After applying the tan, make sure you keep your skin moisturised, to add hydration and help prolong your tan.

12

CHELSEA FASHION

Chelsea fashions are incredible and most of the girls have impeccable taste when it comes to dressing up. I am always looking at the other girls on the show and coveting their designer wardrobes.

Chelsea fashions are incredible and most of the girls have impeccable taste

As you know, I didn't really take fashion too seriously for a long time, after everyone kept saying how they loved the fact that I didn't care. In terms of celebrity style, I love Blake Lively; she is my girl crush. She is so fit and has the best boho-chic style.

I've never really considered fashion to be one of my strong points and when people ask me what they should wear, I always just say that they should dress in the way that makes them feel most comfortable and confident.

My fashion history is a bit dubious, to say the least. As a child, I loved dressing up and, one year, Ba Ba bought me a Snow White dress, with the yellow skirt and red-and-blue top with the heart. I would pose in front of the mirror in it and my

176

brother Ollie would tell me that I looked like a dick, and I would shout at him and tell him that I hated him. He used to tease me and take the piss out of me constantly, but I just worshipped him. Christmas and parties were always a time for dressing up in my favourite dresses.

When I was a bit older, I liked the surfer look and bought hoodies and jeans from places like O'Neill and Quiksilver, but mostly I spent my life in school uniform or in jodhpurs when I was going riding. There have been some proper cringey disasters along the way though. I had one particularly bad knitted jumper, with a big rabbit on my chest, and another outfit I loved was white socks pulled up to my knees over drainpipe jeans, which weren't cool at the time, big white trainers and this ABC jumper. I was a complete geek and wore big round glasses for a long time. Combined with my heavy fringe and braces, this meant I wasn't the best-looking child, by a long shot. After sucking my thumb as a child, I had so much work done on my teeth, to reshape my face completely, and I have six years of expensive orthodontic treatment to thank for my straight smile.

As a teenager, I embraced a slightly punkish look, where I wore my big baggy trousers with a thick silver chain and these spiky gel earrings. Then, when I met Minty and Amanda and they looked so cool in tracksuit bottoms, I tried to emulate their style for a while and just wore tracksuit bottoms and jumpers everywhere.

Before the show started, I went shopping with Gabriella to Topshop, but I wasn't fashionable, so didn't even know where to start when it came to pulling together a suitable wardrobe to look good on TV. I ended up wearing a lot of the sort of clothes I wore at home, like leggings, tracksuit bottoms and off-the-shoulder jumpers, in the early days. I quickly realised that even though they may have been comfy, I needed to up my game, with people like Millie and Rosie on the show. It wasn't a competition, but I didn't want to feel like the tramp. Famously, at the pyjama party in series three, Millie and the other girls wore soft and silky negligees and amazing skimpy underwear sets from Agent Provocateur, and I turned up in my most worn T-shirt and ancient tracksuit bottoms. Everyone loved it and thought it was really amusing, but I felt quite self-conscious and underdressed, and it hit me then that maybe I should start caring more about how I looked. Looking back at old shows, I think I looked awful and overweight. My face was really puffy and my hair was greasy. It was when I was going through the bad time with Charlie and I think I had lost touch with my appearance a bit.

With the realisation that I needed to put more effort into the way I looked, I got in touch with a stylist called Laura, who was recommended to me by a friend, and she took me shopping on the high street. I don't spend much money on clothes. I splash out a bit on bags and jewellery, but that's it. From time to time, though, I do go a bit mad and recently I spent far too much on a beautiful Acne leather jacket. I figure that it is a lifetime investment, so I'm not going to beat myself up about it. If I lost it, I think I would probably just crumble. I want to microchip it!

My mum always says that you look good in a bin bag when you're young and you don't need to waste money on expensive designer gear, which is true. When you're older and need some help to look better, that's when you can start spending more money. That's when I plan to raid Old Bond Street, but for now, I mainly go for the usual high-street shops.

Laura advised me to show off my best assets, my legs, in skinny jeans, shorts and skirts. I don't like anything too tight because I hate my hips, so I wear a lot of casual and loose tops. She taught me how to dress cleverly and passed on tips like not wearing so much black and throwing plenty of colour into your wardrobe. She told me that if I was going to wear a slouchy jumper, I should make sure it's a nice furry one, or has a bit of interesting detailing. She also told me to always wear heels. I love heels or wedges, as they make you look taller.

In terms of accessories, you don't need to spend much money at all. As a teenager, I used to spend hours in Primark, looking through their necklaces and bracelets. You can get some nice bits and bobs there, but you do need to look through a lot of stuff to find them, which can be a bit tedious. If you've got a good eye for spotting great accessories, you're sorted.

I'm not a great shopper; I can find it quite boring. Also, I often find that mirrors in shops make you look amazing and you think, 'Oh great, I've lost weight,' only to get home to your normal mirror and realise that's not the case at all! In the early days of *Made in Chelsea*, I did a really sexy fashion shoot for *Loaded* magazine that was good fun, and I loved the pictures. They were quite raunchy, because I was in just my underwear, but somehow they made me look good. I was on the cover, in a *TOWIE* versus *Geordie Shore* versus *Made in Chelsea* theme. One day I was in Chelsea with Gabriella and we saw a man giving

It was one of the most surreal moments of this whole Made in Chelsea journey them out; it was one of the most surreal moments of this whole *Made in Chelsea* journey for me so far. We made him give us armfuls of copies and handed them out to people as they walked past.

I got my first taste of modelling clothing for a brand in February 2012, when Louise, Rosie, Cheska and I were asked to promote a range of clothing called 'Chelsea Girl' for River Island. We did a fabulous shoot in Paradise in Kensal Green, this really decadent restaurant and bar. Then, a few months later, in June, I modelled a clothing line for a fashion range called Punky Allsorts. I was standing next to the designer – Alayna Salter, or Madame Allsorts, as she calls herself – at a bar one night and when I saw her ring, I thought it was amazing. It looked like a little gingerbread house on her finger. I'm the kind of girl that compliments someone when they are wearing something I like, and I asked her where she'd got it. I was so impressed when she told me she'd made it and owns a business and, before I knew it, I found myself modelling a clothing range for her.

For a long time, I didn't really enjoy fashion shoots, because I felt quite self-conscious, but these days, I love them. I guess the more I do, the more relaxed I am, and therefore the pictures are better. Even now, when I first start a job, I am always nervous, but the more pictures they take, the better I start to feel. I can often see how the pictures are looking as we go along, which boosts my confidence a bit. Feeling all glam and being told you look good is really nice.

After a couple of series, I had a lot of people messaging me on Twitter, telling me they loved my style, which was so sweet. They kept asking when I was going to bring out a range, so when Lipstick Boutique asked if I'd like to design one for them, just after the fourth series, I was delighted. I wanted the pieces to reflect my own individual style and be comfortable and casual and not too flashy, with a few easy-to-wear occasion pieces thrown into the mix.

I wanted the pieces to reflect my own individual style

I had no idea where to start when it came to designing them though, so I took some of my favourite items to the Lipstick Boutique team and we looked at them together, planned items around them and took it from there (www.lipstickboutique.co.uk). I loved seeing the collection when it was finished and it was really cool to be able to wear something that I'd designed – I'd never thought that day would come! We named all the pieces after upmarket places in London and my favourites were a two-part piece called Kensington and Fulham, which are leggings and an oversized shoulderless top with leather arms. It's really versatile, so you can dress it up for a night out or down for the day. I hope that I'll be able to launch more ranges with them.

Get my style: my favourite shops

As I said, I love the high street, so here is a list of my favourite shops:

➡

Topshop (www.topshop.com)
Topshop is great for everything you might need for work or a night out clubbing, and if you are looking for something really special, there is the Topshop Boutique, which sells more expensive one-off items. I could literally spend days in the flagship store on Oxford Street.

 Zara (www.zara.com)
In my opinion, this is the best shop on the King's Road. There is always loads of choice of everything, be it jeans, jumpers, shoes, dresses or bags. The clothes are often really colourful, with interesting detailing, and they have a really unique feel, even though they are from the high street.

 Harvey Nichols (www.harveynichols.com)
Stocking brands from Whistles and Reiss through to Marc Jacobs and Hermes, Harvey Nichols is one of my favourite shops, because after a day of trying on clothes with my mum, we always go to the fifth floor for a glass of champagne and a gossip. It makes it feel like a special occasion and is the perfect way to end the day.

 Primark (www.primark.com)
As a teenager, I used to love shopping here for jumpers, tracksuit bottoms, T-shirts and shoes. It can be pretty full-on, as it's often busy, but if you find something you love, it's worth the effort because the prices are so good.

♛ River Island (www.riverisland.com)
You can get some quality individual pieces in here that are really on-trend and are inspired by the catwalk. It is a great place to go for an affordable head-to-toe look. I loved the collection they did with Rihanna – it was hot!

♛ Oliver Bonas (www.oliverbonas.com)
This shop sells everything from quirky jewellery and unique dresses to interesting homeware and books. They always stock a really eclectic mix of items, so it is a great place to buy gifts for friends.

♛ Ad Hoc (www.adhoclondon.co.uk)
I used to go to this boutique on the King's Road loads with my mum when I was younger. It's really wacky and fun, with sex toys at one end and amazing funky jewellery at the other. It's a real mecca for Chelsea girls.

♛ Kurt Geiger (www.kurtgeiger.com)
I like to step out in style and the heels here are always really comfy and stylish. There is always loads of choice to make a footwear statement on a night out.

♛ Bluebella lingerie (www.bluebella.com)
I love their items because they are really well made and are great quality. They look like Agent Provocateur but they are high street prices.

13

CHELSEA GIRLS DO EAT

Like most girls, I have fat days and often feel crap about my body. When I look back on the first series of *Made in Chelsea*, I hate my appearance; I think I look enormous alongside the likes of Millie. She has got such a rockin' body – what a bitch!

I have hated my hips since I was a teenager. If I could've chopped them straight off with a sharp knife, I would've been delighted. I'd also love to do lipo on my cheeks, if there is such a thing. Sometimes I think I look like a hamster! I'm always told I look better off camera than on, which makes me feel a bit better, because I hate HD cameras. I think they really make you look bigger than you are. I find that flicking through high-end, glossy fashion magazines, like *Vogue* and *Tatler*, seeing pictures of really skinny girls, is really hard, because I'm not one of them.

Doing loads of photo shoots meant that I was always looking at pictures of myself and finding faults. I hate front-on

Like most girls, I have fat days and often feel crap about my body

184

pictures and always want to look skinnier. My mum, who has fabulous curves, has always told me to learn to love my body, hips and all, and I've finally realised that the best way to do that is to accentuate the parts of my body that I like, such as my legs. It's only really in the last year or so that I finally accepted my body and stopped cringing when I look in the mirror.

I've never gone on one of those stupid diets that some celebrities do, like the cabbage soup diet or the one where you drink that weird pepper and lemon juice; that's just not me. I would never be able to stick to it, for a start. If I could look like anyone, I would pick Angelina Jolie. She's the most beautiful woman in the world and everything about her is perfect.

After I split up with Charlie at the end of 2012, my self-esteem was at rock bottom. As a couple, we had always drunk too much and eaten too many takeaways after big nights out. I was living in baggy clothes, drinking my recommended weekly amount of alcohol in a few hours and, after a overindulgent New Year, when I gorged on Mum's cooking and woke up most days with a hangover, I felt awful. Breakfast would be a huge plate of home-cooked fare and every night I would gorge on enormous portions of meat and veg or a pizza. We also went away skiing. We'd live on toffee vodka and have to find a way to get down the mountain, which took some concentration!

I just can't say no to food. I love a good curry; chicken jal-frezi is my favourite. My local curry house delivers up until 12 a.m., which can be pretty dangerous. I love toast with butter and Bovril too. I don't think I was particularly unhealthy – I've never eaten loads of sweets or chocolate, for example – I just ate too much.

When I was offered the chance to go to a boot camp, I jumped at it. I weighed ten stone, the heaviest I had been for a long time. I had heard of these residential places where you basically exercised all day, every day, for a week and completely changed your body shape and your attitude to food. So, not long after going back to London after the New Year, I went to Norfolk to the No. 1 Boot Camp. I figured that if it would help me, then I was up for the challenge. I knew that being locked up for a week was the answer. To say it was brutal would be something of an understatement. We woke at 6 a.m. every day and had to be out on parade in the courtyard area in front of the trainers at 6.30 a.m. It was January and absolutely freezing, so warming up with some exercise was almost a relief.

The programme is designed to push you mentally and physically. The mornings consisted of two-and-a-half-hour-long sessions of cross-training, circuits and high-intensity interval training, where we would get our heart rates really high before resting periodically. In the afternoons we would do military-style hikes of seven or eight miles, to maximise the weight loss. We would then do another session of high-intensity intervals or a stretching session before dinner. After all the exercise, we were supposed to dive into ice baths, to help our aching muscles recover and get our circulation going. I only ever did that once, on the first day – it was awful and I'm not convinced that it really helped.

When I woke up on the second day, I couldn't brush my

hair or my teeth, because my arms hurt so much. I had a massage, to try to ease my aching muscles. After the lady had finished, and I was lying on my front, she put a towel over me and left the room, so I could get changed. I couldn't even get off the bed, everything hurt so much, and I momentarily considered rolling off and flopping to the floor! It was so painful. In the end, I yelled to Lulu, who had come with me and was in the waiting area. Lulu is really sporty and fit, and it was only her encouragement that really kept me going. We shared this old house with all the other people taking part and we were lucky because we had our own bathroom and a shared double room. We took so many hot baths that, in the end, they took the plug off because we were using all the hot water!

The trainers were really professional and the food was good, even though the portions were minuscule and probably half the size of what I would normally eat. We only consumed around 800–1000 calories a day, and were obviously burning off a lot more, hence why everyone who goes loses loads of weight. We had to detox from sugar, caffeine and dairy and we weren't even allowed chewing gum or those power tablets because they have sugar in them. The staff even threatened to search our rooms in case we had any treats hidden away. I learned tricks like putting chilli flakes on my portions to give them an extra kick and more flavour, and it speeds up the metabolism too. I also started to love coconut water, which is great for rehydration after exercise. It takes some getting used to, but it's worth it.

After a week, when I stepped nervously onto the scales, I had lost almost a stone and was back at nine stone and a slim size ten. I felt so much more confident and much happier wearing tighter clothes. After boot camp, I wanted to keep going and continued to lose a bit more weight when I got home. I realised that before I would just eat and not listen to my body when I felt full, so I knew that if I ate slower, my brain would clock when I had had enough. They taught us the trick that if we were good for eight days, on the ninth day we could have a treat and splurge on whatever we fancied, to speed up our metabolism again. It's stupid to deprive yourself constantly; I can't keep going like that.

Other tips I learnt included not having caffeine after 2 p.m. or carbs after 5 p.m.

Other tips I learnt included not having caffeine after 2 p.m. or carbs after 5 p.m. For a while afterwards, I also trained with a guy called Lee Andrew, who helped me keep the momentum going. He got me out of bed in the morning – no mean feat after an evening of filming for the show – and we would go to the gym and do a workout or head for the park for a jog and some interval training. He would also send me pictures of suggested portion sizes.

I tried to stop drinking wine. When I wake up with a hangover, my one cure is always Domino's pizza. I switched to having vodka, lime and soda, because it has fewer calories than wine, but still tastes good – and my hangovers are much better. I also bought my beloved dog Scrumble, a King Charles spaniel, who lives with me in London. I thought he might help me limit my big nights out.

However, like most people, life gets busier and the good intentions don't always last. My weight yo-yos a bit and I find that one heavy night out often leads to carb-rich food and then another night out. Of course I worry about putting on weight as I'm getting older, but I figure everyone has insecurities. For a while, I found it hard to motivate myself to go to the gym after filming, because it can get so boring.

After letting my weight creep up a bit and not doing as much exercise as normal, I decided to go back to boot camp in June 2013. This time I went to the Ibiza camp, which was altogether more luxurious than the one in Norfolk, although they worked us just as hard. It was the same early starts – we would be woken up at 6 a.m. with a blasting rendition of Haddaway's 'Life', this really old-school dance track. If I hear it now, I'm like, 'Noooooooo!' Again, all the trainers were ex-military and really quite scary; there was a lot of swearing and shouting. I think at first they thought I was a spoiled brat, but realised pretty quickly that I wasn't like that and I tried to work hard and get on with it, just like everyone else. By the end of the week, I was laughing and joking with them. A few people quit midweek, as it was so hard.

The heat was intense and we did a lot of walking along the coast, which was really deserted. There were some interesting animals – I ended up with lizard on my back on a few occasions. It's weird, but these boot camps make you quite emotional and tetchy, mainly, I guess, because you are starving yourself. We used to play games in the pool and choose sides. My team was called 'Betches' – and sometimes we did behave like bitches and it would get ridiculously competitive and we would almost try to drown each other for just one point. Once my friend Lulu burst into tears, and I have never seen her cry. It's very testing. I lost a stone in a week and went back down to 9 stone 10lbs, and my body continued to burn fat for two weeks after because we had trained so hard. We only had two hours to chill every day and I spent it relaxing by the pool – that saved me! I felt really proud of myself when I had finished and we all got dressed up on the last day and had a nice dinner together and congratulated ourselves – and each other – on making it to the end of the week.

I think that it's more difficult if you're in a relationship

Since I have come back, I have tried to keep the good intentions up and I aim to go to the gym twice a week, doing classes like circuits, interval training and swimming. I think that it's more difficult if you're in a relationship. In the past I've found that I eat a bit more when I have a boyfriend than I would do if I was on my own. I get really jealous if they have a bigger portion than me. When I first started dating Alex from the show he was doing a 'six-pack' challenge with some of the other boys for *Men's Health* magazine, so he had cut out drink and was eating really well, and I tried to do it with him. We started trying out new dishes and one of our favourites was tortilla pizzas, which we made with tortilla bases, loading them up with tomatoes, chicken, peppers, broccoli, cheese and chilli and baking them in the oven. I try to go out one night a week, and drink vodka, lime and soda and try to resist getting a kebab on the way home and a Domino's the next day to ease my hangover!

My top ten no-diet rules

If you're like me and you love your food too much to go on a proper diet with all sort of complicated dos and don'ts, follow my top tips about how to stay in shape, while still eating what you love.

Take your time

Make sure you sit down at mealtimes and concentrate on the food you are eating by chewing slowly. Try to savour each mouthful – and you'll automatically find yourself eating smaller portions and realising more quickly that you are full.

Load up on veg

Serving three portions of vegetables rather than just one means you will eat more without really thinking about it. The high fibre and water content will fill you up with fewer calories.

Add some chilli

I add chilli flakes to loads of things, like bolognese, homemade pizzas and soups. Apparently there is research to show that adding spices to your diet, especially chilli, can raise the metabolic rate by up to 50 per cent for up to three hours after your meal. And it tastes great, so it's win-win.

Don't deny yourself

I think that by denying yourself your favourite foods, it makes you want them even more. Try to be good – and then allow yourself a 'treat day' every week to ten days, where you eat whatever you want. It gives you something to work towards. I love to treat myself to one of my mum's Sunday roasts. They are amazing.

Watch the booze

An innocent-looking glass of wine or cocktail will add hundreds of calories to your daily quota and, even if you eat well, you will consume more than you realise. I now drink vodka, lime and soda to minimise the damage when I'm out. Also, it might sound obvious, but make sure you drink enough water. If you are having a big night out, drink one glass of water for every alcoholic drink.

Get moving

Part of my thinking when I got Scrumble, my dog, was that it would help me incorporate exercise into my everyday routine. Sometimes staring at a wall while pounding away on the treadmill can get pretty boring, even for the most hardcore gym bunnies. There are plenty of other ways to burn off the fat, without thinking too hard about it: take the stairs rather than the lift; walk rather than getting a cab; or hit the shops with lots of bags, to give your arms a good workout.

Sleep for longer

I love this tip – and my bed! I once read that going to bed thirty minutes earlier and waking up thirty minutes later than you normally do can help you make better food choices. If you're well rested, you're less prone to snack through tiredness or stress.

Have a kick-start

I found that going on a boot camp was a brilliant kick-start to my diet and fitness regime, because I knew I couldn't cheat and had to stick with it. It gave me the chance to totally change my bad habits and start afresh when I came home. I also didn't want to undo all the hard work I'd done when I was there.

Don't skip meals

You may think that skipping meals will help you lose weight quicker, but this isn't the case. Don't eliminate entire meals – especially breakfast first thing in the day – because it will just slow down your metabolism and have the opposite effect, actually making you eat more and put on weight in the long term.

Mix it up

When it comes to going to the gym and structured exercise, try to vary your routine as much as possible, to keep it interesting. If you do kickboxing one day, then do circuit training the next and swimming the next. You will work out for longer and stay more motivated.

14

GIMP MASKS AND CREME EGGS

As the success of *Made in Chelsea* snowballs, I have been lucky enough to be offered loads of opportunities for work outside of the show. Shortly after the show started, I joined an agency and was managed by a woman called Anne, but in November 2011, I switched to an agent called Sean O'Brien, who really looks after me and keeps me busy with work. He looks after Spencer and looked after Hugo, and quite quickly after I started with him, he began getting some exciting jobs through for me.

Now I'm on TV I also get the chance to do a lot of personal appearances. I like coming home to my own bed, although these appearances are often quite a way from London. Normally, Jason, who acts as a tour manager, drives us around. Sometimes there can be so many people pushing in a crowd to catch a glimpse of me or get us to sign something that it can be a little scary. But Jason is brilliant; no one messes with him and he makes sure everyone sticks to the rules, like only hands above the waist for the boys!

I've also been fortunate enough to do some endorsements for brands that I like, which is always great fun. I normally do a photo shoot and then interviews with journalists from magazines and radio stations, to promote the campaign in question. Sometimes I also meet competition winners – and the girls are normally really

I've been fortunate to do some endorsements for brands that I like

lovely and sweet. At the time of writing this book, I have done campaigns for Wrigley's Superstar Smile, Wall's Solero, Cadbury Creme Eggs and SwissAir. They are often more of a privilege than hard work. For SwissAir, I had to stand on an escalator with loads of hot men, and for Cadbury, Louise and I were dressed up in *Mission Impossible* suits and hung from the air, holding spoons, and Louise recreated the iconic *American Beauty* pose and was covered in Creme Eggs. I was given loads of boxes, which didn't help my diet mission, but they were delicious!

In terms of interviews and journalists, you can see them coming from a mile away if they are trying to get secret stuff out of us, but most of the time, I enjoy interviews.

At the start of 2013, Spencer and I were asked to take part in a video for the singer Stacey Jackson and were flown to New York for a couple of days, to film a *Fifty Shades of Grey*-style music video for her track 'Pointing Fingers'. It was shot at New York's Openhouse art gallery. Stacey was really friendly and it was good fun. Spencer had Louise with him and we were put up in a lovely hotel. It was great to have a bit of time to do my own thing and I met up with one of my sister's friends and we went out for lunch and saw some of the sights. I flew home on my own, which I hated. The fact I no longer need someone to look after me makes me realise I've actually grown up!

I've also been lucky enough to take part in a few other TV shows since starting on *Made in Chelsea*. In 2012, quite soon after the show began, I was asked to star in a *MIC Come Dine With Me* for charity, and it was really fun. The other contestants were Caggie, Spencer and Mark-Francis. At Mark-Francis's house, I did come out with a few ridiculous comments, like 'Is risotto rice?' and 'Veal is a baby lamb.' The other guys really took the mickey, so I hoped that would be the only Binky-ism of the week. Safe to say, it wasn't. The voiceover man shredded me to pieces, the little bastard. No one else was rinsed as much as me. Looking back on it, I did say some stupid things, but I sometimes speak before I think.

Caggie's night was 80s themed and I dressed in leggings with a neon headband and sweatbands, like in the video for Olivia Newton-John's 'Physical'. Mark-Francis was particularly over the top that night, but I still think he's great. He is quite ridiculous, but very funny with it. It was a good chance to get to know everyone better. We spent a lot of the week *Caggie talks* discussing whether Caggie and Spencer *a lot of sense* would ever properly get together. I've always loved Caggie; she talks a lot of sense. I was so shattered, because I was still working at LingBridge, so after every dinner, I fell asleep on the sofa!

I was the third one to be a host and everyone came to Lilac Cottage. I decided to do a country-style menu, with mushroom soup to start, roast pheasant for main and berry Pavlova for dessert. Mum did all the shopping and made everything, of course. The camera filmed me wrapping the pheasant in bacon, stirring the soup and putting the topping on the Pavlova, but that was all I actually did. Thank goodness for Mummy! We dressed up in a 'country toffs' theme and I wore a tweed jacket and Cliffy's top hat. Mark-Francis hated the fact that the dogs were around; it was really amusing. Baxter, one of Mum's dogs, was at the table and we fed him while we eating and Mark-Francis was freaking out. Afterwards, we did some welly wanging, which is basically throwing wellies as far as you possibly can, in the back garden. They all gave me nines.

Spencer's evening was the final night. It was a cockney theme and I dressed as a chimney sweep. His food was brilliant and he even made pie and mash with my initials in it. However, while eating it, we

I couldn't believe I was sitting on the sofa that has seen so many famous bums

outed the fact that he had hired a cook to help him. In the end, when the producers totted up the scores, Mark-Francis came fourth, Caggie was third, Spencer was second and I won. I was really happy. Forget *Made in Chelsea*, it's all about *Made in Sussex*!

Another major highlight was appearing on *Jonathan Ross* last year alongside Jamie, Ollie, Spencer and Millie. It was pretty awkward, because Spencer was on flying form, so it was hard to get a word in edgeways, and he kept calling Jonathan Ross 'J-Dog' or something ridiculous. It was a real honour though and I couldn't believe I was sitting on the sofa that has seen so many famous bums before mine. I love Wossy; he is such a legend. We have also been on Alan Carr's *Chatty Man* a few times and he is always hilarious. After one show, Ollie and I went back to Alan's house for a party with him and his partner and it was a really crazy night. He is a genuinely lovely guy. I left a load of jewellery at his house, because Ollie and I got so drunk I completely forgot about it. I saw him the other day, at this Channel 4 event, and he said, 'I hope you're not gonna come and pick up that jewellery, love, because I've chucked it out!' He is my favourite celebrity.

I also appeared on *The Million Pound Drop* with Davina McCall. There is not much to say about that apart from the fact that Hugo is the cleverest person I have ever met and I put the money where he told me to. As a result, we got the most amount of money out of all the celebrities on the show!

As I became more interested in fashion, I also started to get into make-up. The more I got my make-up done for the show and events, the more I started to enjoy experimenting with different looks and brands. In October 2012, I began writing a beauty blog for the *Daily Mail*, which I love doing. We have shot loads of looks now, about everything from combating lines and wrinkles and picking the perfect foundation, to sexy Halloween make-up and how to get the perfect 'grunge glam' look. For each different look, we record a video of me demonstrating how to achieve it. For a long time, I found it quite hard to speak directly to the camera, but the more we do, the easier I am finding it.

My Binky London nail varnishes are now available to buy online (www.binkylondon.com) and on the Ideal Shopping channel. My first range, which I launched in autumn 2013, was called Oil Slick and featured a collection of metallic colours in rich shades of green, blue, gold and purple, which have a petrol-like effect that shimmers. Gorgeous!

How to paint your nails like a pro

Painting your nails perfectly takes time and patience. Manicures are a great treat once in a while, but they are expensive – and you don't have to spend a fortune to have beautiful nails.

👑 Start by removing any old nail polish. One trick to remove old polish stuck by your cuticles is to dip a cotton bud in nail polish and sweep it around the bed of your nails.

👑 Before applying polish, it's important to clip, file and shape the nail, then remove all the dust by rinsing your hands with mild soap and water and dry thoroughly.

👑 Soften your cuticles with special oil, then push them back and tidy up the area by the nail bed, as this will allow you to apply the polish smoothly.

👑 Using a soft emery board, lightly buff the top and sides of the nail, to give you a nice foundation for the polish to adhere to. Be gentle though, because if you buff too hard, you will make the nail look rough.

👑 Don't shake the bottle of varnish, but roll it between your hands, to mix the components. Apply your polish using a soft and clean brush. Make sure you put an ample amount of polish on the brush: too little and you won't coat the nail properly; too much and it will be hard to keep the colour in place.

👑 In smooth motions apply the colour by brushing down the middle of the nail, then wait a few seconds and do the same on the left side of the nail and then the same on the right side.

👑 Let the nail dry completely before adding another layer and then a top coat. This will prevent the colour from chipping or peeling. I love Dior's Gel Top Coat, which gives nails a wonderfully polished and glossy finish.

👑 Finally, once your nails are completely dry, make sure you keep your hands moisturised, so you can show off your handiwork. I love L'Occitane Shea Butter hand cream, and the tube is the perfect size to pop into my handbag. It keeps my mitts super-soft all year round.

15

MUMMY FELSTEAD AND MAKING PEACE WITH DAD

No book about my life would be complete without a chapter on Mummy Felstead. She is an absolute legend. If I am upset, depressed, worried or sad, speaking to my mum makes everything better again. She calms me down brilliantly. If she wasn't around, I genuinely don't know what I would do; she is such a rock.

No book about my life would be complete without a chapter on Mummy Felstead

If I am feeling down, I always go back to stay at Lilac Cottage. We say that when I am broken, she fixes me and recharges my batteries. She puts me on the sofa with the dogs and lights the fire and I sleep for days. I then come back to London and get broken again and have to get back on the train to Sussex, so she can fix me again. When I haven't been back to Lilac Cottage for a while, it's always a good sign. Even though I live in London now, I still think of that house as my home, with all the familiar smells and things around me.

We joke a lot with each other. When things go wrong, I tell her, 'Everything's your fault, because you drank when you were pregnant.' As a kid, I had glasses, grommets and braces, and obviously blame it all completely on her! My eyesight still isn't perfect, but I don't want to get glasses, so I sometimes get migraines.

I try to be generous with her and buy her lovely gifts, and she always reminds me of a story from my childhood. When my grandfather on my dad's side died, he gave all his grandchildren £1000 and, with the money, I bought Mum a £300 video camera. Whenever we argued, I would yell at her: 'And don't forget I bought you a £400 video camera!'; 'What about that camera I bought you for £700?'; 'Remember that camera I bought you for £900!' We talk and joke loads about sex and willies – she is very liberal. Growing up, there was no subject that was off-limits.

She used to struggle to keep me in check, because I was quite naughty and never did what I was told. When I wanted to leave my boarding school, Bedgebury, and live at home, she created a contract with conditions and made me sign it. We still have it at home today. It read:

I will agree to abide by the rules as laid down in this contract and which I have signed on this day.

I. I agree to do my fair share of dog walking and dog feeding. Sometimes this will mean that I will have to walk twice in one day if nobody else is around to do it, on the understanding that this rule applies to everyone.

2. I will not take a can of Coke and leave it only half-drunk.

3. I will not leave any of my belongings in the hall when entering the flat and accept that if I do so, I will take on an extra dog-walking duty

4. I will agree to do my fair share (decided by Mummy) of the washing up and clearing away.

5. I will not assume the living room is mine by right and that I can just lie around in it after school.

6. I will understand that if Mummy has someone arrive and needs me to vacate the sitting room, even if it's halfway through – for example *EastEnders* – I shall do so without a fuss.

7. I will agree to set my alarm each morning and be totally responsible for getting myself up, dressed, breakfasted and to school.

I agree that if this contract is broken, I will suffer in some way, either by extra dog-walking duties, or by making Mummy (who we know is quite wonderful) sad. I understand that these rules are not written lightly, but with consideration, and should be treated with respect.

I was desperate to be back at the flat with her, so I signed it but I somehow doubt I stuck to all the rules.

We speak more or less every day, and she knows that I'm happy when I'm not on the phone all the time. Now things are good for her. As well as being on the show itself, she started her own slot on the 4oD spin-off show, *Mad in Chelsea*. She's quite spiritual and about three years ago she was told by a psychic that in two years from then she would be writing, and now she has her 'Ask Mummy Felstead' column for the *Daily Mail*. She has always been great at dishing out advice. I guess living on your own must be hard, and it gets her out of the house.

She is so glamorous and looks wonderful. The older I get, the more I'd like her to meet someone. I'm still apprehensive about the thought that she could move on, because I don't like change and I'm quite selfish in that I want her for myself, but when I think about being married with kids, I would like for her to have a man in her life too.

She often comes with me for nights out, and always has done. When we used to live together, she would always be propping up the bar with me. Sometimes I tell her, 'Mummy, it's time for you to go home now,' and she always does. She says, 'OK darling,' and I put her in a taxi, telling the cabbie to drop her safely home. I can't completely let my hair down when she's around and get as drunk as I want to sometimes. She loves young company and sticks it out for as long as possible most nights.

> She often comes with me for nights out, and always has done

She got her own keys to my house cut without me knowing. She is quite naughty like that, but I know it's because she worries about me. She loves Scrumble like one of her own dogs and calls herself 'Granny' and looks after him for me when I am away.

Mum has always made my birthdays really special; she often spoils me. For my twenty-first I had a celebration in Sussex and one in London. A month after the show won a BAFTA, I celebrated my twenty-third birthday at the Kensington Roof Gardens in west London, and we had a brilliant night. My ex, Simon, organised it for me; he is very sweet like that. Loads of my friends, family and the cast, like Lucy, Mark-Francis, Ollie and Stevie, came down to celebrate. My manager, Sean, organised for a singer called Peter Aristone to sing. As a joke, he said the backing singers were from the band Mumford & Sons and, obviously, I believed him – I'm so gullible! Gabriella was also there and, at one point, she jumped onstage to serenade my guests too, much to everyone's delight. The party went on well into the early hours and there was a lot of dancing.

Mum and Dad have never made up since their split, but my relationship with my dad is finally starting to improve. Back in 2010, before *Made in Chelsea*, Dad came back into my life. My brother eventually persuaded me to have dinner with him and Dad, and shortly after we stayed at his house a couple of times overnight. It wasn't strange being with Dad again, because my brother

> My relationship with my dad is finally starting to improve

made sure it was upbeat and we all had fun. By then, Dad had started dating a lady called Jette. She is Danish and really different to my mum. She was very girly and wanted to be my friend.

On one occasion, he invited us out for dinner and I knew

something was up because he seemed very serious. He said, 'I need to talk to you about something really important.' He sat us down and told us that he had bowel cancer which had spread to his liver and that it was quite advanced. I started to well up and felt really weird and sad, as did Ollie. Our relationship had been strained, but I have always loved him and I hated the thought of him being ill or in pain.

I started to text him more after that, to ask him how he was, and he would reply, and as he got progressively more ill, I would also go down to Sussex to see him. By that time, he had bought a cottage in a pretty village called Herstmonceux in East Sussex and Jette moved in with him. Sometimes I went with Ollie and he would bring his girlfriend, Lizzie, whom he'd met at the Duke on the Green. He used to go out with Lizzie's best friend's older sister and they met each other on a night out. For a long time, I wasn't sure about her, because I felt really protective of Ollie and selfishly didn't want anyone to take my big brother away from me. I was quite jealous for a while and felt he'd changed. He became less of a player, more serious and would always go home early to be with her. Now they live together and she looks after him, and we get on really well.

Whenever I saw Dad, it was really nice, never awkward, but he would still say things like, 'I hope you're spending Christmas with me this year,' knowing full well that it would be really difficult for me to do that, so I guess the old issues never went away. Sometimes he would also make me feel guilty about how often I went down to see him, and he would rub it in about how close he was with a lot of our old family friends, which I found quite difficult, because I feel that my mum doesn't have anyone.

Last year, Dad married Jette, but I didn't go to the wedding. I know he was upset that I didn't go and I understand why; if I were in his shoes, I would feel exactly the same about the situation. I know they wanted to get married but I just couldn't feel good about it. I could have got it completely wrong, but I'm quite a strong person and I like to stick to my beliefs. I didn't want to have to be a part of it, or be two-faced, so on the day, I stayed away. I saw the pictures people had posted on Facebook, which was odd because there were loads of photos of all the people who my parents were friendly with when we lived in Endlewick House. Everyone looked the same, except older, of course.

I know that Dad watches the show. At the beginning, I think that he and Ollie used to bitch about it, but now I know that Dad is quite excited about how my life has changed since it started and all the opportunities that have come my way. I don't think they ever thought it was going to be a success. He does ask me about it, but he forgets everyone's names, so it takes me a while to work out what he is talking about!

Ollie, Lizzie and I have spent the past couple of Boxing Days with him, and Jette has cooked a meal for us all. It takes time to forgive and forget, but it feels like we are slowly getting there. He has chilled out much more and now often just sits and listens and makes the odd comment or joke. The older we both get, the more I see myself in him. He has mellowed as well and we have a really lovely relationship now.

Our relationship turned another corner at the end of 2013,

when I went to the Royal Marsden, one of the leading cancer hospitals in London, with him and we sat together while he had three hours of chemotherapy. It felt quite strange, and very sad as well. I didn't really understand about the cancer, or what it meant, but one of the nurses explained to me about the tube that went into his heart and the different medicines they were giving him. I'm glad I've got a better understanding of his treatment and his diagnosis now. At one point during the session, he started sweating and felt really sick and I panicked and was pressing the button to summon one of the nurses. The rest of the time, we joked together and had fun for the first time in ages. We talked about loads of things, including the fact that he had recently reconnected with AL and their relationship had improved, which we were both happy about. We didn't talk much about Jette, but I was encouraging him to get a dog, and to oust Jette's cat!

At the time of writing, his cancer is stage four and it's terminal, but I try not to think about what the future holds. It makes me feel really sad that he's going to lose his hair and the fact that he feels so ill. I feel much closer to him. After the session at the hospital, I took him back to my brother's house in a taxi and wrapped him up in a blanket on the sofa and put the TV on. I lit candles and made him a cup of tea and we spent some more time chatting before I left, telling him I would be in touch soon. He sent me a text the next day saying how much it had meant to him, and I feel like we have made our peace.

16

THE OTHER ALEX

In October 2013 I started dating Alex Mytton, my first proper *Made in Chelsea* relationship. For a while Alex had said he liked me, and after we got to know each other better, I started to become more receptive to the idea of us getting together. One night at my flat we had a cheeky kiss, and I knew then that I liked him. He won me over with his amazing eyes – eyes are so important. I didn't talk to anyone else about it for a long time; I knew I needed to let my guard down and so just went for it.

I knew I needed to let my guard down and so just went for it

At the time I felt that maybe it was meant to be because we have exactly the same birthday, so are both Geminis – and are obviously both called Alex. Back then, on the rare occasions my ex-boyfriend Charlie would message me I told him to stop, because I was serious about Alex and wanted to make the relationship work.

Throughout series six, when we were first getting together, it was a really fun time. We went on a trip to South Africa, which was an amazing experience and everyone seemed really happy for me. Soon after that trip, he came down to Lilac Cottage and met my mum and they got on brilliantly. He was the perfect gentleman and she couldn't stop singing his praises afterwards. I met his family too and really liked them. We started to spend an increasing amount of time together because he lives just around the corner from me in Parson's Green. I really trusted him and we loved just spending time together.

For my Christmas present, he bought me a holiday to Goa and we had such a wonderful, romantic time there. We stayed on the south of the island and spent our days chilling out on the sandy beaches and going out for meals. I felt like we were really falling for each other. On our return, we went to Dubai for a few days and it was great – there were never any dramas. I felt like we were really similar people and that we understood each other.

At the beginning of 2014, we started filming the seventh series and when Alex finally told me he loved me, it felt great. I knew I was totally in love with him too, so I was really relieved when he finally said it. However, a rumour started going around that he had cheated on me back in October on a night out in Oxford, when we hadn't been together for long. At first he denied it, and said he had gone to stay with one of his friends on the night in question, but in the end a friend of mine, who knew the girl, told Cheska the truth: Alex had slept with someone else. Cheska then, of course, told me during a night out at Embargo. Alex claimed he didn't remember anything about it and was devastated. I felt horrible – it was just one of the worst feelings. It was really late at night when I found out, so I went to my friend Sam's house and she looked after me and gave me tea. The next morning, I flew out to New York, where Mum was spending some time with my sister. As soon as I walked into the hotel room and saw my mum's face, I broke down into floods of tears. While I was there, I was so confused because Alex was messaging me constantly saying things like, 'I miss you', 'I love you', 'I'm so sorry, I hate myself for doing this to you', 'my heart is broken' – he basically said everything except that he wanted to get back together. I knew deep down that I was so in love with him, and would do anything to make it work between us.

While we were away, Mum and AL did their best to keep my spirits up and we went shopping one day, hung out at Soho House and did some touristy stuff. I talked about what had happened with Alex constantly – to the point where I think my family got a bit sick of it. AL wasn't really saying what I wanted to hear, while Mum was telling me that if Alex wanted it to work enough, he would come back to me. I think my mum knew all along that my relationship with Alex would never last the distance. As hard as I tried to keep my mind off it, it was almost impossible for me to switch off because every time I tried, another text message would pop up on my phone. It was like he just couldn't leave me alone. One day we

While we were away, Mum and AL did their best to keep my spirits up

211

were at Soho House, and the three of us piled into a photo booth and had some funny pictures taken and, for one moment, I was laughing so hard that my stomach muscles ached and I forgot about it. But then, when the evening came round, I got tired and tearful and couldn't stop thinking about Alex cheating.

I ignored Alex's messages until the day I flew home. I had come to the conclusion in my own mind that if he had made just one mistake and was really sorry for what he had done, then we could try and work through it. I texted him asking if he still wanted to make it work and he replied saying that we would see what happened when we saw each other, so I knew he was undecided. Yet, at the same time, he was sending me pictures of our holiday in Goa and reminding me of the good times we spent together and telling me that he wished that it had never happened. It was like he wanted to know that he could still have me, but he was unsure if he wanted to be with me. I had never been cheated on before then and had no idea where my head was at – I just knew that we had this amazing connection. He had his own key to my house, and while I was away, he had come to pick up some things. When I got back, I saw that he had taken one of the playing cards that we had taken with us to Goa and had written on it, 'I'm so sorry, I love you' and left it on my bed. I just couldn't understand how he could do that and yet still avoid answering the question about whether he wanted us to be in a relationship.

Filming that scene in my room when we first saw each other after I got back was terrifying. I remember waiting for him and hearing his footsteps coming up the stairs. My heart was hammering and my hands were shaking. As soon as I saw his face, I could tell by his eyes that he wasn't going to try and win me back. Of course, you probably will have all seen the conversation in which he told me that he didn't know what he wanted. I was desperate for it to work and afterwards I was in bits. I hadn't felt so awful since I had broken up with Charlie.

The next day, my mum came and picked me up and I went down to Sussex with Fran, my friend Gemma and her baby. We went on lots of walks with the dogs and went to a little village shop that sold crystals and gemstones. I bought a whole bag full of crystals, which were all supposed to help my love life and make me feel more balanced. While I was away, Alex continued to message me and although everyone was telling me to tell him to get lost and leave me alone, I just couldn't bring myself to do it.

Back in London, I had a girls' night out with Lucy, Cheska, Louise and Stephanie at Upper West. They were all being really amazing and tried to cheer me up, and we had a few drinks. While I was in the loo, Alex came in with Ollie Proudlock and Lucy went up to him to ask him why he was there and defended me. In the end, he left and I was disappointed because I wanted to talk to him so I could make sense of his decision. Afterwards we went to Ping and on to another club, where Alex was out with Jamie. I saw him as soon as I walked in and I was so angry. I felt like he owed it to me to explain his behaviour and I was gearing myself up for an argument with him. I was getting so upset that, in the end, Alex said he would take me home. We got a bottle of wine on the way back and sat up for ages talking. Of course, one thing led to another and we got together. In the morning, I was angry with myself, but it felt so normal to be with him. We took Scrumble for a walk in Bishop's Park and went to our normal breakfast place, Tinto. I felt really happy and relaxed for the first time in ages. Alex continued to tell me that he couldn't remember anything from the night he had cheated on me. Of course he did remember, because it later transpired that he had also slept with three other girls – but more on that later!

We spent the whole day together and he left that evening. No one knew about it, although I think Lucy had guessed because she called me and was really quiet on the phone. The first person I told properly was my mum, when we were at the Hollywood Arms, breaking the news by saying we 'held hands'. I was really nervous about telling her because I knew she would hate it. When the rumours were going around, he looked her straight in the eye and told her he hadn't cheated on me. Normally she's really good at telling if people are being truthful, but she didn't see it coming either, so she felt really hostile towards him. Looking back, I was never going to listen to her, because I had to learn it for myself, but I hated seeing her so upset. I was so blinded by the things Alex said – he was so convincing. Alex knew he had a lot of making up to do – not just to me but also to Mum and to my friends. However, I hoped that the dust would eventually settle and we could all just try to move on.

I was so blinded by the things Alex said

Of course, things are never that simple. When I told Lucy at netball that I was giving Alex another chance, she knew that he had cheated on me with another girl, not just the one I knew about. She had found out that Alex had asked his friend to leave the hotel room they were sharing in Edinburgh because he had a girl with him. Lucy has been through a lot of difficult relationships and has been cheated on before, so she could see the pattern emerging. When she told me, it began to feel like one blow after the other. I remember messaging his flatmate on Facebook, asking if it was true, but he kept ignoring my question. In the end, he told me that I would have to ask Alex myself but he referenced a girl, so I knew there had been a girl involved. When Alex admitted it, I was furious and, of course, really upset. He told me that he hadn't been honest because he *did* want to be with me and he thought that if I knew the truth, I would never take him back. He also admitted to the fact that he had kissed two other girls, but kept saying he didn't love me at that time because we had just started going out. When I asked him to swear on my life that those two times were the only times he had cheated, he did.

I was starting to get so paranoid and sometimes, after he had been for a night out, I would check Twitter and see people had written things like 'Mytton is clearly not smitten with Binky' and 'Binky, you should really think about finishing with Alex after his behaviour last night'. I would screenshot them and send them to Alex, demanding to know why anyone would say that, but he just claimed that people wanted to stir up trouble for us.

In my head, I was taking it slowly and wanted to see what would happen. I still loved him and, for a while, it felt like we were getting back to normal again and over the worst. The girls were really supportive, but I think Lucy was getting frustrated that I wasn't listening to her advice. The boys, of course, kept trying to tell us that us getting back together wasn't a good idea. At the time, I didn't understand why everyone had to have an opinion about my relationship. As far as I was concerned, it had absolutely nothing to do with them.

The girls were really supportive

The trust was gone between us, but I was still determined to give the relationship a chance. In my head, he had cheated on me before we were properly in love, so we were back to kissing and cuddling in public and behaving like a normal couple. At Stevie's party at the Phene, I knew something was up when Lucy and Louise walked over, and the expressions on their faces spoke a million words. The news that Alex and Spencer had had an orgy hit me like a ton of bricks. Alex tried lying again but he couldn't keep it up. There were three girls and Alex and Spencer involved, and eventually I saw some pictures of the girls on Twitter. What happened to girls sticking together? I don't think I've ever felt so angry in my life. My face was burning and when I slapped him, apparently you could hear it down the street! I have never felt so numb and blank. I went and sat with Lucy, Louise and Rosie. Louise knew exactly how I was feeling, after being cheated on so many times when she dated Spencer, so she made sure I had a drink in my hand. From there, we went to Rosie's house, stopping off at Waitrose for supplies, and we sat around her table for hours, bitching about boys and what Alex had done.

During that time, Alex must've rung me fifty times and I kept putting the phone down on him. I had messages from his flatmate, begging me to listen to him because he was so upset. This time he was saying he would do anything to get me back. He was literally begging me.

In the morning, I knew I had to dump him because it had gone too far. He had seen me bawling my eyes out in the bedroom after I learned about the first time he had cheated on me, yet he had still managed to do it again. That morning a big bunch of flowers arrived on my doorstep, and then he sent some Japanese food from one of my favourite restaurants, Sukho. I just felt sick and numb. I couldn't believe he had done that to me – after everything he had said to me about wanting to be together, and me being the only girl for him. When we met on the Embankment, it was very emotional. He was saying we were soulmates and how he had never felt like this before. I was totally exhausted. He told me he would try every day for the rest of his life to get me back and would do anything.

True to his word, this time Alex did try really hard. He started leaving me a red rose every day outside the front door but I still refused to see him. Alex's flatmate messaged me and told me that he had put pictures of us together all around his room. Alex also continued to message me all the time, saying he loved me. One day, he asked me whether I would be at home and I told him I was there with my friend Lulu, but that I didn't want to see him. The doorbell rang, and I sat with my hands over my face. Lulu came back in with this black photo album. Alex had printed off loads of photos of us together, from when we first met and under each photo he had written these really funny captions. It was very sweet, and it broke my heart when I saw it. Lulu and I were both in tears reading it; I know it doesn't sound like a lot, but that album meant everything to me.

In April, a few weeks after I had found out about the orgy, I went to Italy for the launch of my Binky London nail polish range at a tradeshow with Mum, Ollie and my agent, Sean. While I was there, this guy came over with two bottles of perfume and told me they were from Alex. He said he was one of Alex's best friends from University and that Alex had pleaded with him to find me and give them to me. He told me that Alex had been on the phone in bits and begged me to hear him out. I thanked him for the present but told him that there was no way would I hear what Alex had to say. Everyone was telling me to ignore him, but I found it so, so hard. As well as messages, he was sending me videos telling me how much he loved me. He had thought of everything.

On one of the nights when we were in Italy, we went to an Irish bar where I had too much to drink. Everyone else had left ages before me and I got totally lost on the way home. I had no idea who to call and eventually ended up phoning Alex, who managed to get me back to the hotel safely. When I got back to London, I agreed to see him and he took me for a picnic in Richmond Park with Scrumble. He had thought of everything; there was food and champagne and we talked for ages. It was then that he

Everyone was telling me to ignore him, but I found it so, so hard

218

told me he wanted to be totally honest and that the two girls he said he had kissed he had actually slept with. By then, I felt it could get no worse. I had no idea how I should be feeling – I still felt so confused about it. After the picnic, Alex drove us around London and played this mix tape full of songs he knows that I love and some new music. The sun was setting and we had the roof down. London was looking so beautiful and I thought that maybe, despite everything that had happened, we could try again.

From then on, we continued getting back to how it was before. We took Scrumble for walks, and talked and laughed like we used to. It was around this time that things started to go a bit sour with Lucy and Cheska. I didn't want to tell Lucy the truth, because I knew she wouldn't agree with what I was doing and Cheska told people I was upset with her for telling me, which I wasn't at all. I just wanted to concentrate on my relationship, and I expected my girlfriends to be there through thick and thin and to just support me, whatever my decision. During that time, Lucy and Cheska became incredibly close and I found it really hard because it felt like they were ganging up on me. I knew they hated Alex, and Fran was also making it difficult because she lived with me, yet she really disapproved of Alex. I couldn't see the wood for the trees and I felt like I had no energy for anything except trying to make it work with Alex. I started growing closer to Rosie and Louise during this time; Louise understood exactly how I felt because of her experiences with Spencer and Rosie just minded her own business. She said what everyone was thinking – that Alex was an idiot and she didn't like him – but that it was my relationship and I had to do whatever I wanted. That's what I would've said if one of my girlfriends was going through what I was. I would never have turned my back on a friend, regardless of how stupid they were being. In terms of his mates, I had told him that I didn't want him going out with Spencer and Jamie, but I did let him go out and drink. I just wanted him to call me and keep in touch with me and, obviously, come home. He asked for my spare key again, so he could come home to me and he even suggested sending me a picture of himself back at home, so I knew he was really there. One night I even let him go to a strip club; I just didn't want him going out with the boys on the show.

Looking back on the seventh series, I feel quite embarrassed about how it all panned out and how I behaved. My head was just a mess. The reaction from the public was quite hard to take because everyone was telling me to finish it and that I should listen to the girls on the show. I had always said to myself that I never wanted a relationship on the show, and it was quite strange seeing it all played out on the cameras.

I was really excited because I had never been to Paris or had a boyfriend who had pulled out all the stops

One morning just before Easter, when Alex and I were in Tinto, he asked me if I had dropped something on the floor and when I turned around he had put a card on the chair, which said 'Paris tomorrow?'. On the one hand, I was really excited because I had never been to Paris or had a boyfriend who had pulled out all the stops like that, yet on the other hand I still wasn't sure how I felt about everything that had happened. I was nervous about my mum's reaction because she was planning to come to London to cook lunch for some of my friends and me.

Alex and I took the Eurostar to Paris, but before we even got on the train we had an argument about something, so we sat in silence and it felt really awkward all the way there. The hotel was quite sweet but the weekend didn't pan out as I hoped, and I felt really depressed. We saw some of the sights and went to the Louvre, and in the evening I got really dressed up for a night out at one of the traditional cabarets. I put so much effort into how I looked but Alex didn't even look at me or tell me that I looked nice. As we took a cab to the show, I had my sunglasses on but I had tears running down my face. We watched the show and ate our meal in awkward silence and afterwards I started crying and told him I wasn't sure I could get over it. He kept apologising and telling me he was trying, but I think deep down at that moment I knew the relationship was doomed and that I would dump him.

17

NEW YORK, NEW YORK

In the run up to travelling out to New York to film a special series of the show, I was still with Alex and trying to ignore the fact that it was never going to work out between us. I still felt really paranoid and unhappy all the time but I knew there was nothing he could say any more to make me feel better about the situation. The New York trip had been on the cards for a few months and we had talked about living together once we got there. I was really excited about spending some

I was really excited about spending some time in a new city

time in a new city for a while; I hoped it would be a fresh start and give me a bit of perspective on what had happened. Alex and I also thought living together and spending all that time together in each other's pockets would be make or break for us. By then, Alex was practically living with me in Parson's Green, so we didn't see that it would be any different just because we were in another city. It was decided that he was going to come out a few days later than the rest of the cast. However, he started to suggest that if he was going to remain in London, then I was going to have to stay with him, which I didn't like at all. He was making me feel guilty about it and sending text messages asking why I wasn't going to wait for him and questioning whether I loved him. I insisted that I was going out with the others, no matter what.

In the run up to the trip, there was one day when the pressure he was putting me under really got to me. I just felt like I had to escape Alex and London. My friend Lulu lives on the Isle of Wight with her fiancé, Matt. My ex, Charlie, lives there too and they are still all really good friends. When I told Lulu on the phone about how I was feeling and how Alex was being, she told me to drop everything and go there for the weekend. It was a Friday, and completely on the spur of the moment I packed a small bag and decided to go. Alex was livid with me, telling me that all my friends would tell me to leave him, and he was angry that I was going to see Charlie again because he knew how much the relationship had affected me. I didn't care what he said though; I knew I needed some time away from him.

As I caught the train down to Lymington, Lulu texted me a mysterious message telling me that someone would pick me up. At the end of the text message, she put a winky face, so I guessed it might have something to do with Charlie. I was right; Charlie came to pick me up in his speedboat and had really dressed up for me in a white shirt, which was really unlike him. As soon as we arrived, we went for a drink at the

Yacht Club, where we sat outside on the seafront, watching the sunset. The first thing he did was ask me if I was still with Alex. He looked me in the eye and told me I was being an idiot and deserved so much better. That's when it really hit home that I couldn't go on with my life like that; I needed to dump Alex, however painful it would be in the short term, or I would never be properly happy. No one else could make me listen like Charlie could. I still felt that old spark of chemistry between us, but I didn't want to bring myself down to Alex's level and cheat on him. I was very aware that I still had a boyfriend and how I had been treated. We talked for ages, and everything Charlie said really made sense.

From there, we went and met all my other friends and went for more drinks at the Hut at Colwell Bay. Everyone was really happy to see me and, for the first time in ages, I felt really content and relaxed; just like the old me, before I had started dating Alex. I told Alex by text that I had arrived safely and I would speak to him later, but even after everything that had happened, I didn't get a reply until three in the morning because he had gone to a house party with his friends. He had ignored me all night and it just confirmed what Charlie and I had talked about: I couldn't trust Alex and that I would never get the trust back. I was so angry that I told him I was turning my phone off and I wouldn't speak to him until I got home. I had finally had enough.

I had finally had enough

When Sunday came around, I felt really depressed about going home because I knew I finally had to dump him. I messaged Alex telling him it was over, but I knew we had to speak face to face. He sent message after message, pleading and begging, but I just ignored him. The morning after I got back, he came round to my house. I had collected all his belongings from my room and put them on the table in a pile and when he saw it he went crazy. I knew I had to stay strong and I told him that the relationship was making me a psychotic mess and that I could no longer live like that. He was really, really upset and was crying. Eventually after I had said what I wanted to and he knew that my decision wasn't going to change, I hugged him and he left and I could hear him crying as he walked down the road. But despite the fact I felt rotten too, as soon as it was done I felt so relieved and like a huge weight had been lifted off my shoulders. Shortly afterwards, my mum came round to make sure I had followed through with my promise to finish things with Alex and also to help me pack. Amazingly, I managed to take far less luggage to New York than the other girls, but I planned to do lots of shopping while I was there!

We were going to be in New York for two months and since my plans to live with Alex had fallen through, I stayed a night with my sister who lives in an apartment in Soho. She has made a great life there and has met some brilliant people. Her art is going really well – she does a lot of reportage stuff from special events and she illustrates magazines. We met at Grand Central station, and there were loads of people crowding round thinking we were famous because they saw the cameras filming us. I know AL was really nervous being filmed at first, but as soon as she got into it she was fine! She was really relieved that I had finally seen sense and it was great to know

I would have some family support while I was away. She really helped me settle in. My sister was one of a handful of new cast mates – the others were New Yorkers Billie Carroll, Alik Alfus, Jules Hamilton and Carson Eisenhart.

I ended up living with Louise and Rosie in a three-bedroom apartment in Midtown, while the boys – Spencer, Jamie, Proudlock and Stevie – were living in the Meatpacking District, which was a bit trendier. Cheska and Fran were living just down the road from us on Times Square and Lucy shared with Riley nearby, on Park Avenue. Victoria and Mark Francis were also out there.

I was so happy we could all be friends again Not long after I arrived, Proudlock had a house party and I made up with Cheska and Lucy. I felt really upset about the fact that I had fallen out with them, and I wanted to start afresh and put the past behind me. I said sorry for the way I had behaved, tried to explain what I was feeling at the time and that my head was a mess. I never want to fall out with any of my girlfriends over a boy ever again. Both of them were really understanding, and I was so happy we could all be friends again. I had really missed seeing and speaking to them both, especially Cheska. We have always been there for each other through everything. At the same party I also spoke to Jamie, who said that he would be there for Alex. I was really upset that he seemed to prioritise his friendship with Alex over me. I know I shouldn't have been surprised, but I still was and I felt really hurt by him. I felt I had lost a friend over Alex.

Alex did come out to New York in the end. I found out

when he called me, asking for us to meet up. I just couldn't understand what he wanted and as far as I was concerned we had nothing to say to each other. I didn't want to see him or talk to him; just hearing his voice on the phone made me feel tearful and brought it all back again. I was hardly going to feel good about him staying with all my friends, and be happy about the fact he was going to try and get with loads of girls right in front of me and that I was going to hear about it all the time. I wanted him to get on with his own life and leave me to get over the relationship. I felt frustrated and angry, yet still had all these butterflies in my tummy because I couldn't help but still have feelings for him. It felt like I had gone two steps backwards; I had been fine when I was there on my own.

On the night of Cheska's leaving party – she was going back to London for work with Fran, and was having some drinks to say goodbye at this cool bar called the Back Room on the Lower East Side. Alex told me he would be waiting for me in Central Park. At first, I was convinced that I wasn't going to go and meet him, especially as everyone else was telling me that it was a bad idea. I don't know at what point in the evening I changed my mind about seeing Alex, but eventually I caved in and decided I just needed to get it over and done with.

As I approached the fountain in Central Park, where we had agreed to meet, my hands were shaking. I felt sick with nerves. Alex gave me the old 'I'm here with the boys, I just want to have fun and I want us to be friends' chat. I just couldn't believe his attitude; what did he want me to do? Just forget about the fact that he had ruined six months of my life and turned me into a psycho? It was as if he wanted me to be his new wing woman or something – it was a complete joke. I told him that I had nothing to say to him and I didn't want to see him. I wanted him to get out of my life and out of the city. I actually had a real sense of empowerment finally because I knew that I was making the right choice. For so long, I had done myself such a disservice by trying to stick by him.

Unbeknown to me, at the party, Jamie had received a text message saying that Alex had got with his ex while we were all in New York. Jamie was understandably really angry and upset about it because she was his first love and I think he still really cares about her. While we were talking, Jamie came up behind us and asked to talk to Alex. He confronted Alex about what he had heard, but of course Alex denied it until he was blue in the face. Obviously no one believed him. Jamie was distraught about it but, in a strange way, I felt relieved that everyone could finally see Alex for the liar he is. He claimed to love me, yet cheated on me on numerous occasions, so why should he show any loyalty to his friends? He tried to make it up to Jamie but he was having none of it. Rightly, Spencer was clearly sticking by Jamie's side too, so it looked like Alex was going to be pretty lonely during his stay.

In the end, Alex went home after a few days which was the best thing that could happen all round. I found out when I travelled with Cheska and Fran to drop them at the airport. As I was getting into the car to leave, I saw Alex standing there with his suitcase. I just stared at him and got in the car, and we drove off. I felt so happy that he was going; I would no longer have to see him or hear about what he was doing. After that we didn't speak, and on a couple of occasions he messaged me asking me how I was, which just made me really upset. I knew it wasn't worth it, and I cut off all connection with him. I felt utterly broken by everything that had happened. It meant that I could just try and have the best time possible without Alex in the background. Not long after Alex left, Jamie came round to our apartment to apologise for putting Alex first. He just kept saying sorry and that he had been an idiot and had got his priorities mixed up and, of course, I forgave him. I could see that he had really learnt a lesson and I value our friendship too much to hold a grudge.

Living in Midtown wasn't quite as cool as being in some of the other areas and I found it quite difficult not knowing where anything was – I'm not great with change. I think the other girls found it easier because they grew up in the city. I ended up getting taxis everywhere! *I loved living with Louise and Rosie* The apartment was gorgeous and I loved living with Louise and Rosie – there was never any bitchiness or issues between us. We all really looked out for each other. If you've seen the series you'll know that Louise and Rosie started hanging out with Jules and Alik a lot at the beginning, so sometimes I was on my own during the day, but in the evenings we would all go out for dinner together and meet up with other people. We also didn't feel like we had to spend every second together, which was good.

We spent a lot of time relaxing – eating, having fun together and partying. They free-pour alcohol over there, so it was very easy to get drunk on one or two drinks. I used to hang out on the rooftop of Soho House with Louise and Rosie, and on a couple of occasions Spencer and Jamie came as well. A lot of the venues out there are really cool and relaxed, much like being in Chelsea.

Mark Francis and Victoria took me shopping one day, which was fun. Their taste is a bit different to mine because they always look so smart and elegant, while I prefer the casual look. I really wanted to buy myself a bag for my birthday – a present to myself – and, in the end, I found this beautiful tote bag in Celine when I went shopping with Rosie. Rosie is particularly fashionable and shopped a lot and sometimes I would go with her. I went out there with one bag and came back with three, but Rosie went with three and came back with six!

We spent a couple of weekends in the Hamptons too. The first time we went to Montauk – it was me, Spencer, Jamie, Lucy and Riley. It was a really last-minute decision after we had filmed my birthday party; we just decided to hop in a cab and go there. We stayed at this great hotel called the Yacht Club. Billie had rented out a house with her friends for the summer and was already out there, and we had a great time partying with her. The next day I went on a pedalo on the lake with Riley to try and get rid of my hangover – the water always makes me feel so much better. It was a bit of bonding time for us. She is a really great girl, so it was good to get to know her better. From there, we went to a place called the Surf Lodge, which had a live band playing on the beach and really cool vibes. There were loads of hot people around and we danced the day away. Afterwards, we went to a club called the Sloppy Tuna (weird name!) and everyone was roasting marshmallows on the barbecue on the beach.

It was a black barbecue, and because it *We danced the* was dark I couldn't see it and walked into *day away* as I was trying to roast a marshmallow, burning my leg. Jamie suggested I got into the sea, but I think that made it worse. I did go to A&E but the wait was so long that I left. I now have a big mark on my thigh and I think it might scar.

The second weekend I went to the Hamptons, I was with Riley and Louise was going out with Alik. When Spencer and Jamie found out, they decided to gatecrash! We filmed a scene at Alik's parents' house in the Hamptons, which was beautiful. After dinner, we played lots of silly drinking games and were a bit hungover in the morning, but a big American breakfast with waffles and Buck's Fizz soon sorted us out!

It was great that AL was there, and I saw her at least once or twice a week. For my birthday, Mum flew out and we went to the James Hotel and we celebrated on the rooftop bar, which is called Jimmy. I told my Facebook friends that I was having a party and loads of friends who I haven't seen for ages randomly turned up, which was great. My sister told me to buy a bottle of vodka for everyone – it turns out it was $1000! I got so drunk that I ordered another bottle because I kept pouring it into everyone else's glasses. In the morning when I saw the receipt I nearly had a heart attack – I've never spent that much money before on alcohol! In some ways, it felt like a fitting end to a really rough time. Another thing we did in my birthday week was life drawing. Rosie, Louise and I met up with my sister, who gave us an art class at a studio on the Upper West Side and who had organised a hot male model for us to draw. We were crying so hard with laughter it was like none of us had ever seen a willy before. Rosie was snorting, which made me laugh even more. I felt a bit sorry for the model but we just couldn't stop laughing. I also had another birthday party, which was filmed and for that my sister had flown out Gabriella Ellis from LA as a surprise. I had no idea what this big surprise was – I was terrified it would be some sort of old, dodgy pop star. When Gabby turned round from the stage area and started singing 'Empire State Of Mind', I was really happy to see her. I haven't seen her since she left the show and I love her songs and her music. It took me back to the early days on the show when she lived in London. It was a glorious evening catching up.

Of course there was romance for the boys

I was quite happy being single while we were out there and not looking for anything. It was really good to reconnect with the boys again after everything that had happened. I felt like everyone was really looking out for me.

Of course there was romance for the boys – both Spencer and Stevie were trying to get with Billie, which was quite amusing, and Louise and Rosie found romance.

The time went past so quickly and, before we knew it, it was time to come home. We finished our time there with a big wrap party in Brooklyn with all the camera crew and the New

York production team, who we had been working with. On our last day we packed up all our bags – Rosie needed a lot of help with hers – and we toasted our time there and the series with champagne. It felt quite sad in a way, but I was really happy to come home and see all my friends and family again. It was an amazing experience, but I was delighted to be back surrounded by my home comforts. Mum had been looking after Scrumble for me while I was away and I spoke to her loads on the phone and Facetimed when I could. I even Facetimed Scrummy! I was so happy to see him again! My sister Minty had had a baby while I was away – Cosimo, who I arranged to see as soon as I could after I got back. He is just beautiful (and a fellow Gemini!), and I also went to the Isle of Wight and saw Lulu and Matt. It was mostly a weekend for wedding organisation because they are engaged and I am their bridesmaid, so we wrote lots of lists and made plans. While I was there, I also saw Charlie again, which was fab, as always. I don't think anything will happen romantically with Charlie, but I'm so glad he finally made me see the situation with Alex for what it was. He will always be a great friend.

Looking back over the New York series was a completely different feeling to watching the seventh series. I watched the second episode when Alex left New York with some friends and family, and everyone cheered when I got in the taxi and left. My mum was yelling, 'At last!' Everyone was so ecstatic about it! Watching it back, I was relieved that I finally felt I was being myself again and rather than being against what I was doing, the show's fans were also happy I had finally seen sense. People were saying stuff like 'Binky's back!' on Twitter.

The series was shot so beautifully I don't know where I went for a while there. The series was shot so beautifully; rather than fast cars and Victorian properties, it was an amazing montage of the incredible skylines, the busy streets with yellow taxis and the famous backdrops, like the Statue of Liberty, Brooklyn Bridge and Central Park. I'm so grateful to be part of a show that is so beautifully produced.

I finally feel like I'm over Alex and what has happened. I don't miss him at all and I am really happy being single. I have seen him once since our encounter in Central Park, when I bumped into him on the street in Chelsea. He asked me if I was dating anyone and I said no, which was true, but in my head I was thinking that it was absolutely none of his business. I thought I would be really upset when I saw him but I wasn't really. I have no interest in having anything to do with him. I've decided that I want to have a relationship with a proper man; I need someone who is really going to look after me.

At the time of writing I'm just about to head back to Sussex to be a bridesmaid for one of my friends, and I've got two friends called Adam and Matt moving into the house, which I'm really looking forward to. They are really cool, fun guys. I used to fancy Adam when I was about thirteen. He worked at Wingrove House with me and would drop me off in the evenings after my shift. Obviously we're just friends now, but I can't wait to have some male company in the house again. I feel like I've turned a corner and I'm finally in a really good place. Long may it continue!

My top New York hangouts

Soho House (www.sohohouseny.com)

The rooftop here, which overlooks the Hudson River and Downtown Manhattan, has a swimming pool, sunbeds and a bar. I hung out here a lot during the days when I wasn't filming. On Sundays it was particularly popular and by 8 a.m. all the sunbeds would be taken, so we tried to get up at 6 a.m. and would rush there with our bikinis and towels to make sure we bagged one. On a couple of occasions we managed it, but the other times we had to hang around and wait for someone to leave and then pounce! We would have a few drinks and sunbathe and it had a great vibe.

Bloomingdale's (www.bloomingdales.com)

One of the most famous department stores in New York, a trip to Bloomingdale's is an incredible shopping experience. It takes up a whole block of real estate on the Upper East Side of Manhattan and is the perfect place to begin shopping in the city. You could probably find anything you were looking for here – from high-end designer fashions, through to mid-priced home ware.

The best time to visit is in the mornings on weekdays because it is less crowded.

Central Park (www.centralparknyc.org)
The park has some great memories for me because it was here that I told Alex to get lost and out of my life. It's 843 acres in the heart of Manhattan, so it's also very hard to miss! There are loads of things to see and do here, such as taking a boat ride on the lake, seeing Central Park Zoo and checking out the romantic Bow Bridge. It's really leafy and green and feels like a little slice of countryside in the city.

Empire State Building (www.esbnyc.com)
This famous 103-storey skyscraper in Midtown Manhattan is where we did the press shoot for the series, which was great fun. It goes without saying that the views are incredible – it's a must-do for any visitor to the Big Apple.

TAO (www.taodowntown.com)
This restaurant in Downtown has a club-like feel and is known for its huge Buddha centrepiece and trendy crowd. Cheska, Fran, Louise, Rosie and I had a fab evening here.

CATCH (www.emmgrp.com/restaurants/catch/)
Mum, AL and I ate at this contemporary American seafood restaurant, which is based in the Meatpacking District, one evening before Mum went home. The food was insanely good. I ate loads of spicy prawns and delicious fish – it was one of the best meals I have had in ages!

Jimmy Rooftop at the James Hotel (www.jameshotels.com/new-york/bar-lounge/jimmy)
This is where I had one of my birthday celebrations and it was amazing. The bar also has a rooftop pool with loads of wood decking and sexy outdoor showers. I was very tempted to jump into the pool after I had one too many drinks but, thankfully, I didn't!

Yankee Stadium (http://newyork.yankees.mlb.com/nyy/ballpark/)
Cheska, Fran and I went to watch a baseball game here. We got those massive foam fingers, which the Americans call 'weeners', and caps. It was one of those traditional things I wanted to do. I didn't really understand what was going on or much about the intricacies of the game, but the crowd went crazy and it was a really amazing atmosphere.

MOMA (www.moma.org)

Louise dragged Rosie and me to this modern art museum for a look around one day. It has a huge collection of paintings, sculptures, films, photographs and drawings – and although I can't say I am a massive art fan, it was really fun in the end and we had a good time.

Avenue, Chelsea (www.avenue-newyork.com)

This is where I had the birthday party, that AL had organised. It's a great club venue with two storeys, and an enormous dance floor and an amazing vaulted ceiling. They have also hosted private events for the likes of Marc Jacobs and Kim Kardashian – so I was in good company!

THANK-YOUS

Gosh, where to start? Putting this book together has been a brilliant experience and I've had a great team behind me, but I'm going to try to keep it short and to the point because, given a free rein, I could go on forever. Thanks to all my friends, family and fans ... you know who you are.

Mummy, you are the best, most supportive mother in the world. Thank you for looking after me through life's ups and downs. It will always be you and me.

To Ollie and AL, for being the best big brother and sister I can possible think of. I love the fantastic memories we have shared together and look forward to many more.

To Minty and Amanda, both of you coming into my life was the best thing that could have happened to me. You are blood to me and I couldn't wish for a better extended family to join the Felsteads.

Daddy, I'll always love you.

To Sarah Dillistone, David Grainger, Heidi Birkett, Mo

Mohsin, Ros Coward and everyone at Monkey Kingdom, thank you for giving me the opportunity to star in Made in Chelsea. I have finally found a job which I adore!

To my old friends Letty and Lulu for always being there for me.

And to my great new friends – Cheska Hull, Ollie Locke, Lucy Watson, Spencer Matthews, Rosie Fortescue, Fran Newman-Young, for many, many good times.

To Sean O'Brien, thanks for looking after me and for all your help and support and to Mark Fuller at Sanctum Soho for getting me in on the guest list at his amazing parties. Thank you to Rakesh Aggarwal at online beauty retailer Escentual.com and Siobham and Sinead at Glo Fulham.

To my fabulous editor Carly Cook, thanks for believing in this book and being brilliant to work with from day one. And to the team at Simon & Schuster, including Abigail Bergstrom and Hannah Corbett for making the book possible. A round of sambucas on me!